RIVER BIRDS

RIVER BIRDS

BIRD LIFE FROM MOUNTAIN STREAM TO ESTUARY

ROGER LOVEGROVE
& PHILIP SNOW

FOREWORD BY TONY SOPER

COLUMBUS BOOKS
London

(*Author's dedication*) FOR INGELA

(*Artist's dedication*) FOR MY PARENTS, JASON AND THE TAO

First published in Great Britain in 1984 by
Columbus Books
Devonshire House, 29 Elmfield Road, Bromley, Kent BR1 1LT

Text copyright ©Roger Lovegrove 1984
Illustrations copyright ©Philip Snow 1984

British Library Cataloguing in Publication Data
Lovegrove, Roger
   River birds.
   1. Water birds—Great Britain
   2. Freshwater biology—Great Britain
   3. Marsh fauna—Great Britain
   I. Title   II. Snow, Philip
   598.2941   QL690.G7

   ISBN 0 86287 093 3

Designed by David Fordham

Production in association with Book Production Consultants, 47 Norfolk Street, Cambridge

Typeset by Cambridge Photosetting Services, 19–21 Sturton Street, Cambridge

Origination by Anglia Graphics Ltd, Bedford

Printed and bound in Yugoslavia

CONTENTS

FOREWORD

Roger Lovegrove is exactly the right man for this book. To explore riverscapes from source to sea you need a knowledgeable and companionable guide; every page reflects his enjoyment of the endless fascination of waterside. Rivers have so much to offer all of us – anglers, day-trippers and committed birdwatchers alike, to say nothing of their resident wild communities. What may at first glance seem to be a scene of calm and serenity will, on the most casual investigation, reveal high levels of activity among the residents: kingfishers excavating their nests, dippers patrolling their beat, swans keeping a watchful, if disdainful, eye on human visitors, herons preparing to grab an unsuspecting fish, mallard preening their waterproof plumage . . .

The artist Philip Snow has brought vivid and brilliantly observed illustrations to the printed page. These place the birds in their typical habitats and illuminate their different characters. Only an artist who is also a dedicated bird-watcher could achieve such standards of excellence. The pictures also serve to reflect the changing moods of the landscape through which the river passes – from bleak, rain-soaked mountain-tops through tranquil, verdant lowlands to, eventually, the wide-open expanse of an estuary at dawn.

In recent years rivers have been the subject of a great deal of investigation, survey and research, and the importance of their continued healthy existence recognized. More and more of us are aware of the threats posed by the march of both agricultural and industrial events, and want to see action taken to preserve our natural heritage while the opportunity is still there. Roger Lovegrove and Philip Snow remind us in this timely book just how much is at stake – not just for those of us who are 'in the trade', not just for committed birdwatchers, but for everyone.

Tony Soper

INTRODUCTION

Rivers are remarkable phenomena, too often taken for granted by most of us. The world over, countless rivers and streams carry mountain rainfall back to the sea, where it evaporates to become water vapour and, eventually, rain once again. Each river forms an essential part of this cycle, irrigating on its journey the valley which it has itself formed and supplying it with soils brought down from the hills. No single factor on Earth has had a greater influence on man's colonization and ability to survive than the existence of fresh water in these rivers. Man, like so many other species, has evolved to cope with amazing extremes of heat, cold, discomfort and barrenness provided only that fresh water is available in some form or other. Thus throughout the passage of time man's evolution has been strongly determined by water courses on their journey to the sea; in some parts of the world (the Nile valley, the rivers Tigris and Euphrates, the Punjab, for example) whole civilizations have developed in linear corridors in river valleys, wholly dependent on the reliability of the river's flow.

Britain's rivers and their valleys have been an endless source of inspiration for poets, writers, painters and composers. When one considers the great variety of wildlife which our rivers provide and the exquisite beauty of many of them, such ability to inspire is not difficult to appreciate. In our modern technological world, however, so much is available to us at the press of a button or the turn of a tap that it is easy to forget the part that rivers play in our daily lives. Not only have they determined the locations of most of our cities, towns and villages, but they have also significantly influenced the form of the countryside around us; they still directly supply our water needs in most areas, provide for a substantial part of our outdoor recreation and serve as transport for our effluent.

Accordingly, each of us sees the river in a different light: what is aesthetically satisfying for one person may be an unwelcome hazard, a planning problem, a recreational opportunity or an engineering challenge to others.

Certainly for the naturalist and birdwatcher the riverside provides opportunities probably second to none in terms of variety and numbers of birds and animals, and also in the relative ease with which such wildlife can be seen, by virtue of the river's narrow linear nature. It is my hope that this book will open the door for those who have not previously realized the immense wealth of bird life to be found along the lengths of rivers; for those already familiar with these birds I trust the book will help promote a fuller understanding of them and act as a reminder of their infinite variety. Demonstrating this variety are the beautiful illustrations by Philip Snow, an artist whose work is rapidly becoming well-known and who is clearly going to make his mark in the field of bird art and illustration as the years go by.

I have tried in the following pages to trace the course of the river – a notional river, albeit I refer often to the Severn as the archetype – and its birds from source to mouth, from the mountains in which the major rivers rise to the estuaries where they empty into the sea. The plan of the book reflects the classic stages of development of a river. It rises in the heights of the hills, drawing its waters from the whole saturated sponge of the mountainside; in its highest channels it will then fall away off the mountain in gradients so steep that it often flows directly over bedrock and is frequently characterized by vertical waterfalls and steep-sided gullies and valleys cut by its own erosive force. Once off the mountains the gradient is less steep, although the river still runs fast: cataracts, riffles and boulder sections predominate and the river begins to leave behind the heaviest of the rocks it has chiselled from the mountainside.

As it leaves the uplands altogether its character alters again. Meanders develop once the river wanders across the plain; the V-shaped valley it has cut through the hills is also left behind. Much of its cargo of pebbles and larger-grained sediments is dropped now as it crosses the lowlands, providing material for innumerable shingle spits and islands. It is now a shifting river too, frequently cutting a new course through the soft alluvium. By the time it reaches the estuary only the finest sediments remain, in suspension, colouring the water and replenishing the rich fertility of the intertidal areas.

This is the classic course of a river, though it does not necessarily apply to all of them. For example, many of the streams in the lowlands of southern England originate within the soft chalk hills, often first appearing as springs on the hillsides. Such streams do not have any of the characteristics – or the birds – of the mountain streams or torrent sections; they are perhaps the poorer for it, for their range of birds is restricted to those associated with lowland sections.

There is one other concept which I am anxious to convey to those who delve into this book: the concept of what we should understand as constituting 'the river'. I refer not to its length or depth but to its sphere of influence. Almost any river influences an area well beyond the limits of its banks. An obvious example is at times of flood when the river itself may be many times its normal width; but at other times, also, the river has direct influence over a broader area – an area at least as wide as its immediate valley floor. Here, on the water meadows and fields created by the river's deposits, birds and other wildlife – breeding waders, yellow wagtails, amphibians and wetland plants – are true functions of the river and the water table it creates on the land round about it. In Chapter One I try to illustrate this concept at the river's source too.

There is a battle on our riversides. Ultimately, this battle is about the eventual shape and form of our rivers, and its outcome will substantially determine the future content of the wildlife which they support. On one side are those who, for reasons of sentiment, scientific integrity, pastoral recreation or visual amenity would see rivers remain as nearly pristine and unadapted as possible. On the other side, answering to the ceaseless call for more and better agriculture, as well as the need for flood prevention, are the powerful regional water authorities. Their river works and land drainage operations are aimed at providing well-drained fields in the flood plains and a speedy and unimpeded passage for the water in the river channels. Such works are almost inevitably detrimental to most forms of riparian wildlife and each individual project makes further inroads into this resource while simultaneously changing the appearance of the rivers through grading banks, straightening channels, removing bankside vegetation or clearing trees. Great efforts are being made to moderate the steps the water authorities take, through both legislation and persuasion. The authorities are not unresponsive, although the overall effect of their work all over the country is deeply depressing. One authority at least, the Severn-Trent Water Authority, is now committing itself to carrying out reconstitution work on river banks and it is hoped that others will follow.

This book is written for those who seek to enjoy the bird life on our rivers. If it in any way succeeds in awakening consciousness further and thereby serves to help the cause of protecting our rivers and their invaluable wildlife I shall be doubly happy.

Roger Lovegrove
May, 1984

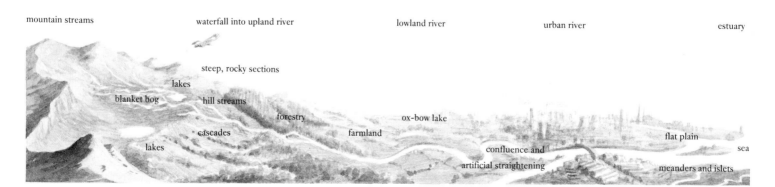

mountain streams   waterfall into upland river   lowland river   urban river   estuary

steep, rocky sections

lakes

blanket bog   hill streams

forestry

ox-bow lake

cascades   farmland

lakes

flat plain

confluence and

sea

artificial straightening

meanders and islets

RIVER SOURCE

Previous pages: carrion feeders predominate among the limited range of birds equipped to live at the river's source.

The Plynlimon mountain lies brooding in the heart of Wales, looking down westwards on the little towns of Aberystwyth and Machynlleth and the sweet, long curve of Cardigan Bay. Its massif straddles the waist of Wales, not as an imposing buttress of mountain but as a great rolling complex of plateaux rising aimlessly to their five heads (Plynlimon means 'five heads') and to an undramatic summit ridge of 2,427 feet. It is a lonely and forbidding place inhabited by red grouse, peregrine, raven, kite and only a handful of other birds.

On a grey December day at the turn of the year the rain marches, column after column, across the flanks and shoulders of Plynlimon, swept in from the Atlantic and the Irish Sea by a relentless wind. The wind buries itself in the western slopes of the mountain, swirls through the gullies and rocks on the windward side and drags the heavy clouds in curtains of rain uninterrupted across the open hill. It rained yesterday too, and will probably do so tomorrow; 250 days each year it rains on Plynlimon and empties an annual depth of nine feet of water on the quaking bogs and sodden mountain pastures; small wonder that two thousand or more mountain streams and rivulets spring from its sides.

THE BIRTH OF THE RIVER

Mighty rivers are born here on this mountain of everlasting water; the Wye on a scenic course south, the Rheidol plunging westwards in a short but spectacular rush to the Irish Sea, Twymyn and Dulas to the north and Severn, greatest of them all, at the start of a long curve through the heart of England towards its outlet in the surging tides of the Bristol Channel.

Through the sweeping curtain of rain a raven calls twice in a deep, throaty croak, '*prok, prok*', as it lifts off from the rotting carcass of a mountain sheep huddled below a peaty overhang by one of the tiny streams. Two carrion crows, sleek, wet and malevolent, move in to take the raven's place. Coal-

Ravens are successful camp followers of the sheep flocks on the high hills where the river has its source.

12

black birds all of them, their demeanour and their purpose fit the brooding atmosphere of the day, for even here at such a time life must go on; if this is where the raven and the carrion crow will find their food then this is where they must be. Certainly this is no day for a birdwatcher on the open hill; a day on which only a rain-blurred glimpse of raven or crow will be seen in exchange for the soaking wetness, the cold and the possible dangers of the open mountain on a wild winter day. Exposure can overtake you fast and without warning in these conditions. However, if we are to know the full story of the river and of its birds this is the place to start. Moreover today is exactly the type of day when it is easiest to understand the origins of the river and also to appreciate its true form in these highest reaches.

Carrion crows are menacing, wily and unpopular, but they profit well from the toll of wildlife casualties in the hills.

For here at the place of its birth the river does not conform to the tidy image normally conjured up of an embryo stream suddenly springing from the earth and sliding busily downhill on its course. In fact the river is unseen, but spreads everywhere around us and below our feet. If we keep still we may hear its water coursing through tiny veins underground; move, and we can feel the river in the wet ground moving too. Here the whole mountainside, its bogs, its soils, its rivulets and its plants are the river, lying like a huge sponge which, when squeezed by further falling rain, leaks its precious water into myriad streams lower down the mountain. On a wet day like today this is self-evident: running water is everywhere. The sky is full of it and the peaty ground, sodden to capacity, can hold no more. Across the whole mountainside every tiny runnel and rivulet, every sheep-track and gulley runs with water; each heathery overhang and peat bank drips and the howling wind tears and plucks the droplets off the waving strands of purple moor grass and rushes and tosses them again downwind.

HILLSIDE COLOUR

Yet even in dismal weather there is an abundance of colour. The drier shoulders and ridges are covered by dark banks of dormant heather; the russet red stems are bared to the wind and the grey-green of lichens can be seen on many of them. Beside the heather banks is the wetter blackness of the exposed peat on the dissected plateaux of the watershed. In the bowls of the little valleys lie the wet bronze patchwork of last year's rushes, the pale gold of driven banks of molinia grass and the brilliant emerald-green of treacherous mossy bogs. The sheep, dotted across the hill, are washed an almost dazzling white by the incessant rain.

So here, in the bogs and hollows of Plynlimon, the Long River is born. This mountain massif is only one of many in the wet hill areas of the north and west of Britain, where so many of the great rivers have their source. Fed by the unfailing rainfall, the heather moors of the Pennine Chain give rise to the Tees, Tyne, Eden, Ribble, Trent and a host of others. Dartmoor and Exmoor are the birthplace of most of the short, fast-flowing rivers of the

south-west, and the high-rainfall areas and vast peat flows of the uplands of Scotland produce the many Scottish rivers.

Many, if not most, of these areas are formidable places for birds. Those which live there are either highly specialized (golden plover, red grouse, common sandpiper) or can cover great distances to find the food they need (golden eagle, red kite, raven).

THE SOURCE OF THE SEVERN

On the eastern slopes of Plynlimon at its identifiable source the Severn does not spring dramatically from the ground as might befit the longest of Britain's rivers. Instead it emerges shyly, in an unpretentious trickle, amongst rushes and bog mosses. Predictably, the spot is named Blaenhafren ('the head of the Severn'). For the hardy walker or birdwatcher a well-signed Forestry Commission trail leads to it, running for several miles through the conifer plantations then out on to the bleak slopes of the open hill. A short distance to the south, over a shoulder of hill, the groundwater parts company from the Severn and seeps into the source of the Wye. From here, over a course of 200 miles, the Severn will descend the 2,000 feet to sea-level near Gloucester. En route it will cross the heart of central Wales and wind through the rich agricultural plains of Shropshire, passing as it does so the very cradle of the industrial revolution, spawned on its banks and fuelled by its waters. It will sweep through the majestic cathedral cities of Worcester and Gloucester before pouring under the wide span of the Severn Bridge and emptying its mountain waters into the Bristol Channel. As it does so it is reunited with its sister Wye close by the Severn Bridge, a meeting of waters which parted over 200 miles and one week earlier on the misty hills of Mid-Wales, where they mingled on Plynlimon and had their sources a mere two miles apart.

RIVER-BIRD SPECIES

Across the country other rivers do the same. Throughout the course of these rivers some eighty or ninety different species of birds will nest along their banks, or on their islands, ox-bows, riverside trees or water meadows. Others will feed in the food-rich waters and the lush vegetation on the banks. All these rivers – Avon, Derwent, Ouse, Tyne, Thames, Severn or Trent – are rich corridors for wildlife in the diminishing wetlands of Britain. They support and sustain a great diversity of insect, animal and plant life and are among Britain's most valuable bird habitats. For birdwatchers these are justifiably popular and rewarding areas – not least, for those who dare, the far reaches in the hills.

Rainfall may be heavy and frequent but many winter days are bright and clear enough to tempt the birdwatcher into the hills. Although the number of birds which use these bleak areas in winter may not be great the quality for the birdwatcher is good. This is also the best place in which to see several species with are otherwise difficult to encounter, such as raven, red grouse, buzzard and kite.

The red kite is exclusive to the river valleys and hills of Central Wales.

A few other specialist birds of prey exploit smaller birds and mammals in the mountains.

As ever – especially in winter – it is food supply which determines where birds are likely to be found. The bleak open hill has relatively little to offer at this season. Insect and invertebrate food is virtually non-existent; the main sources of food in these upper parts of the river system are carrion and vegetable matter in the form of shoots and seeds of aquatic plants, when the upland pools are not frozen over. A few species such as peregrine, hen harrier and merlin will spend some of their time hunting in the hills in these barren months, but most of it on lower land; the number of birds that can rely on this habitat at all seasons is very few indeed.

RED GROUSE, RESIDENT OF THE OPEN HILLSIDE

Only one species, the red grouse, is a true resident of the open hills all through the year. A vegetarian bird which feeds entirely on the young shoots of heather and buds of bilberry and cotton grass, it has no option but to remain where these plants grow. Through the short days of winter, even in the bleakest conditions of snow and frost, red grouse are found on the sheltered banks of heather and on the drier ridges above the bogs and rivulets. Only they can subsist through the long months of winter on the modest nutrients of the summer's growth of heather shoots.

On many of the keepered moors of northern England and Scotland red grouse occur in prodigious numbers, artificially protected and nurtured by the activities of keepers to produce a surplus for the August and September shooting parties. In Wales these days of former glory are almost gone as grouse moors give way to forestry schemes, conversion to grassland or simple neglect through failure to keep the heather in good condition.

There is one time in their lives when these game birds are not strictly vegetarian. When the young birds hatch in May and early June the adults take them down off the heather to the wetter patches in the bogs and banks of stream where they are fed on the glut of mid-summer insects. These are rich

The red grouse is the only bird which remains the whole year round on the heather moors.

in protein and much more productive of rapid growth than the vegetarian diet to which the birds will progress after the first few weeks, and on which they will remain for the rest of their lives.

On the Welsh hills however it is the carrion-eating birds which rule supreme: red kite, buzzard, raven and carrion crow all profit from the sheep casualties on the winter hills, and none more so than the raven.

At no time of year is it necessary to walk far along a mountain watercourse on Dartmoor, Wales, Lake District or Scotland before hearing the sound of ravens. These parts of the country are their great strongholds and they are commoner here than anywhere else. Seemingly oblivious to cold or vile weather, they winter happily in the highest hills feeding on the readily available carcasses of sheep and other carrion. Together with the red kite and the carrion crow they are the classic British carrion-feeding birds. The raven, shyest but strongest of the three, is the largest of the crow tribe, half as big again as a carrion crow, with a huge chisel bill that enables it to open a carcass with ease. Only when the raven has had its fill and moved aside will the smaller crows take their turn. Sheep carrion forms a crucial part of their diet throughout the year and they are heavily reliant on the continuance of sheep farming in the hills. On the Plynlimon and on plenty of other mountains in the north and west, sheep rule and there is no shortage of food for the raven, but in some river catchments where the wholesale afforestation of the hills has replaced upland agriculture the raven has been lost, for he cannot feed where new forests cover the ground and sheep no longer graze. Northumbria and south-west Scotland are two areas where for this reason raven numbers have reduced dramatically over the past two decades.

The ravens have a subtle relationship with the mountain streams which takes two very different forms. First, they continually search the hills for ailing

RAVEN, SHYEST OF THE CROW FAMILY

Ravens nest on the crags above the mountain streams and display aerially from mid-winter onwards.

sheep, which often perish, waterlogged and weighed down, in gulleys and runnels from which they are too weak to extract themselves. A knowing birdwatcher will often follow the line of watercourses, either tracing them with his binoculars or by using them as his main route. Frequently these too are the places that will yield the few other birds on the hills at this season.

RAVEN NESTS ON CLIFFS AND WATERFALLS

Also, where the mountain stream has cut a deep-sided course in the soft rocks the raven will build its nest on the resulting crag. Many sites of this nature are found in the high hills, often beside a waterfall and always skilfully sited under the shelter of an overhang. Sometimes the great wool-lined stick nest will be built in the thin branches of a twisted rowan growing, secure from sheep, directly out of the cliff itself. Year after year the birds will add more sticks to the nest and re-line it. Such sites are easy to pick out from a distance, because the cliffs will be a slimy green below the nest where the rock is streaked with algae. Many of these stream-side nests are very ancient, and are kept in use year after year: individual ones are known to have been occupied for fifty, even sixty, years or more, and indeed the birds themselves may well live for this length of time.

The raven, denizen of these stream valleys and hills, is in every way a winter bird. From early winter the pair – they partner for life – will start to call and display high over the river. In the crystal air they fly together, calling *'prok, prok'* in a deep, resonant and throaty voice. As they cross the hillside the male rolls in the sky, flipping on to his back, continuing his straight-line flight upside-down for a few yards and then rolling back again.

Although faithful to their hill retreat they will readily move further afield to join others at a special source of food. In areas where ravens are numerous it is not rare to see a hundred or more feeding on the carcasses of sheep washed down by the river in flood or at the heaps of offal outside slaughter houses. Near the little town of Llanidloes where the Severn flows off the eastern foothills of Plynlimon ninety or more congregate daily at the municipal tip, where they consort with as many as 400 carrion crows.

RED KITES HUNTING THE HILLS

The tiny remnant population of the beautiful and elegant red kite is restricted in Britain to the hills and valleys of central Wales. In winter the kites, often roosting communally in specially-favoured woods, will travel great distances to search for carrion during the day. Like the ravens, kites are scavengers, relying heavily on sheep carcasses; they will wander far, as many as eight miles from the roost, in search of food. They travel with almost languid ease, circling with their long, broad wings gently bowed, above the river catchments and steep-sided valleys, then planing across the hillside and out of sight with barely a beat of their wings. With deft wings and flexuous tails they are marvellously agile fliers when the need demands, infinitely more nimble than, for example, the common but clumsy buzzard.

Kites hunt the high hills during the day and roost – sometimes communally – in the valley woodlands.

18

Having found a carcass, the kite must rely on the more powerful raven to open it up, for though large the kite is not strong in this respect. It is actually quite unusual to see a kite in occupation of a carcass, for much of its feeding is achieved by piracy – harrassing crows and magpies as they leave the feast.

IN SEARCH OF KITE

Red kites are highly prized by birdwatchers and many travel to Wales each year in the hope of catching a glimpse of these rare birds. Most come in spring and summer. However, this is not the best time to see them, quite apart from the risk of the birds being accidentally disturbed during the nesting season. Winter is the season to find red kite. Then they not only congregate to feed at regular favoured places, but they also tend to roost communally in particular river valleys. Once, on a cold, clear January day, four of us saw fifteen kites hunting the foothills or circling the great bog at Tregaron, where the river Teifi spreads across its broad valley. Then we went to one of the steep, wooded valleys in the hills behind Aberystwyth, on the edge of Plynlimon, to look for birds coming into roost. In the next hour at least twenty kites flew down into the valley from the surrounding hills, sometimes singly, sometimes in twos or small groups. At one point nine of the graceful birds were in the air together, six in the view of the telescope at one time.

Not only did birds pass above us, but they glided leisurely over the little fields sloping steeply down below the road, following the course of the river, dipping and twisting in slow motion over the meadows and weaving through the ancient oaks on the valley side. Their colours glowed in the afternoon light, russet, brown and white. That afternoon was no exception; the kites are there each day in winter.

A host of small pools and lakes are scattered across the wet hollows in the heart of the river's source. The waters are of course cold; they are naturally acid, too, the complete opposite of the chalk streams of southern England. This means that there is poor development of plants and other potential food for birds and therefore they are usually unattractive to waterfowl. In winter however, when cold has not covered the lakes with ice, goldeneye are often here, plump, solitary and tireless ducks with brilliant yellow eyes; the males, which appear to be black and white, have a distinguishing white patch at the base of the bill. They come from the far north in winter, from breeding areas in the great conifer forests on the lakesides of Scandinavia and Russia (small numbers now nest in Scotland too). They dive into the icy waters of mountain pools apparently ceaselessly and oblivious of the cold. Their meagre diet consists of molluscs and crustaceans which they hunt on the stony lake bottom, turning over stones with their bills to free the larvae and invertebrates beneath. Often there is a handful of tufted duck too, and sometimes pochard, riding on the wind-chopped surface in a tight group or duck-diving from the surface to hunt the bottom of the lake eight or nine feet below for a variety of plant and animal items. Occasionally a party of whooper swans will stop over or a group of goosander will grace the lake, plumbing its depths for fish, but just as often it will be deserted – flat, calm, moody and reflective under the shadow of the mountain.

WINTER DUCKS ON ICY POOLS

On one of the more peaty lakes by the source of the Severn wild geese come to stay in the late part of the winter. They are white-fronted geese from Greenland, special in that this small flock of sixty or seventy birds, together with one other little flock half its size on the watersheds twenty miles further north, are the only Greenland whitefronts to be found in the whole of England and Wales. The world total of this northern goose is no more than about 12,000 birds and in late summer the whole population migrates to western Britain to winter mainly in County Wexford, and on the goose-full island of Islay in the Inner Hebrides. The larger of the two modest-sized Welsh flocks spends most of the winter on the coastal marshes of the River Dovey and resorts to the hill lakes and bogs in March and April, while the smaller flock appears to spend most of the winter high on blanket bogs moving from one mountain lake to another.

ARCTIC GEESE ON THE WILD WINTER HILLS

These birds, which breed on the tundra plateaux of western Greenland, spend barely three months on the Arctic breeding grounds, squeezing their breeding season into the brief hundred days of summer thaw before being forced south again. Necessarily they are amongst the first winter visitors to arrive in Britain, and will then spend some eight months awaiting the long journey to the farther side of Greenland again.

On the Plynlimon bogs the geese are difficult to find. Although they are large birds their plumage is dark and they merge well with the sepias, ochres, black and tan of the peak bogs. Wild geese are amongst the wariest of birds, too, and they resort to areas where their panorama is wide so that only the most skilful and cautious birdwatcher can approach them. They feed here on the nutritious roots of cotton grass, the bulbils of white beak sedge, deer sedge and moorland grasses.

All these then are the rewards for the intrepid birdwatcher at the source of the river in winter: birds which are few in number, but special because they are so scarce. They are often seen in circumstances of weather, light and mountain mood that will produce a memory far more lasting than that of the mere reward of finding the birds themselves.

RETURN OF THE SUMMER BIRDS

How different is the story in the spring and summer! Now the boggy river source is alive with bird activity. All those birds which deserted the hill last summer as soon as their last broods were on the wing have now returned. The insect harvest has begun again and there is food to be had. Both the grassy hills and the heather moors ring with the insistent calls of meadow pipits and their graceful parachuting display flights. Skylarks, too, are singing high above the hillside, and crouched low in the heather the red grouse now sits hard on

White-fronted geese from Greenland are the only geese to make use of the hills in winter.

her precious clutch of eggs. Improbably, the lake which harboured diving duck and winter swans in the most uninviting part of the year is now deserted save that on its stony shore a pair of common sandpipers, highly strung and constantly agitated and alert, feed delicately and nervously. They hunt by sight for both adult and larval insects hidden amongst the shingle of the shore line, and are adept at advancing stealthily with head crouched low to dart and make a quick snatch at stationary stonefly or damsel-flies.

Their nest is hidden, difficult to find in the tufts of fescue grasses above the stony sides of the lake. They move ceaselessly as they feed, bobbing dipper-like all the while; if an approach is too close they fly with flicking wings and short glides low over the water to the next promontory. Here the male watches, still bobbing and calling an oft-repeated 'pitti-wee-wit, pitti-wee-wit, pitti-wee-wit', the summer call of the waterside in these raw hills.

Where the emerald-green mosses betray treacherous spots amongst the boggy areas there are reed buntings. These birds are more numerous in the lower stretches of rivers but here they breed in scattered pairs dotted across the wetter parts of the catchment. They have a nest of woven grasses and stalks in the depths of big tussocks of sedge and rush. The male advertises his presence with a short jingling flurry of song. He is bright and conspicuous as he sings, perched swaying on the rush heads, but his song is thin and strangely out of place up here in the hills.

In the wettest part of the bog lies a small, deep, treacherous-looking pool where the waters of the hidden river show themselves briefly on the surface of the moor. The pool is no more than fifteen feet across and its quaking margins are alive with the gently waving heads of cotton grass and rushes. Its surface is utterly black and still; the only movements in its waters are the trembling reflections of the fluffy white cotton-grass heads, bending in the

The upland lakesides and streams are enlivened by the arrival of common sandpipers in April.

Pairs of reed buntings breed in wet, rushy bog areas.

slightest breeze. Unseen in all this stillness, a bird is there, watching and crouching among the pondweed leaves and overhanging rushes. Against the poolside a drake teal, small, compact and alert, eases closer to the bank; his smallest movement is sufficient to betray his presence, causing tiny ripples which spill gently across the surface. This time camouflage alone has not been sufficient; the approach has proved too close for comfort and, alarmed, the teal springs high in the air and takes off in a frenzy of rising wings, steepling rapidly above the bog. He circles wide; two minutes later he is down again three hundred yards away on another pool, deep in the safety of the river's quaking mosses. His presence is proof that not far off, in dry tussocks just above the wetness of the bog, the duck teal, drab and chequered and therefore better camouflaged, is sitting tight on her clutch of eight or ten eggs. Alone she undertakes all the incubating, leaving the nest daily to feed on the pools of open water or in the shallows of the bigger lakes nearby. When she leaves the nest, she carefully covers the eggs with its downy lining to conceal them from the predatory eyes of carrion crow, raven or black-headed gull.

BREEDING TEAL IN THE BOGS

Together with meadow pipits and skylarks, the reed buntings are the only species in the huge order of passerines (perching birds) which have learned to adapt to the harsh and restrictive environment of the open hill. Ring ouzels may occur in the valleys and gorges running off the hills and grey wagtails frequent the streams themselves, but otherwise these three species alone have managed to exploit the open hill. Only one other can lay claim to intruding into their domain, the ubiquitous wren – an unlikely inhabitant of this area. From sea coasts to mountain slopes the wren prospers in a wider range of habitats than almost any other species. An insect-eater, it manages to eke out an existence in the peaty overhangs and scree slopes of the mountainsides.

Apart from the occasional pair of mallard nesting in the drier banks of heather, teal are the only wildfowl to breed on these remote and lonely bogs. Food is sparse in these acid areas and the teal survives by virtue of a catholic diet. During the winter in their lowland flocks they are almost exclusively seed-eaters but on the breeding moors they feed on a wide variety of items which include vegetable matter, aquatic insects, the larvae of flies and midges, and small crustaceans and molluscs if available, as well as the seeds of many water plants. Much of the feeding takes place at night, which is the safer time to leave the nest unattended. The tiny ducklings, newly hatched, feed for themselves immediately, mainly on a diet of insects and insect larvae in the early days, and are then brooded by the female at night. The male, once mating has been completed, takes no further part in the functions of breeding and rearing the young, and it is most frequently the unattended male which is to be seen – or even a group of three of four loafing their way through the summer months on the hills.

The black-headed gull is another breeding inhabitant of the inaccessible (to the birdwatcher) parts of the river's source. It is an interesting bird whose life-story is characterized by several contradictions and misconceptions. To start with, it does not have a black head at any time of year, but in spring develops the dark chocolate mask which gives it its misnomer, relieved only by a narrow white orbital ring; after the breeding season the brown feathers are moulted out and the winter birds have nothing left of the patterning save a dusky spot behind each eye to remind us, and to help identify the winter birds from others of the family.

Neither do these small and graceful gulls necessarily conform to the popular image of 'seagulls'. There are many individuals which both breed and live on the coasts all the year round and others which resort there in autumn and winter but, alone amongst Britain's several gull species, plenty of black-headed gulls probably never have the need to go within sight or sound of the sea.

Such birds will nest on these high, remote bogs and lake-islands in the hills. They feed on farmland and open waters in the lowland river valleys, sometimes taking advantage of the inexhaustible supplies of urban man's waste on municipal refuse tips up and down the country.

As early as January some of the adults begin to show signs of the chocolate head in preparation for the breeding season. By April the birds are back on the breeding sites in the hills, resplendent in their spring plumage. Here they will nest either in the moated sanctuary of the peaty islands in the hill lakes or in the fastness of quagmires of floating vegetation on lake margins and in quaking bogs. Except when they resort to a favoured lake or reservoir in the hills for roosting in winter – often in their thousands – they use these places

The teal is the only duck which regularly breeds in the bogs of the river's source.

purely as safe breeding sites; for food, they have to commute to the fertile areas in the lowlands.

Black-headed gulls return to their hill colonies in April.

Black-headed gulls are one of the success stories of our time: in the last century they became so rare through the gathering of their eggs for food that there was a genuine risk of their extinction. The change in their fortunes was so great that by 1973 the population in England and Wales alone was in excess of 100,000 pairs. The story has been similar in other west European countries: in the Low Countries numbers rose from about 60,000 in 1950 to over 220,000 pairs by 1978, and in West Germany (especially Bayern, Baden-Wurttemberg and Schleswig-Holstein) numbers have risen by probably over 70,000 pairs in the same period.

GULLS ENLIVEN THE HILLS IN SPRING

When the gulls return to the hills in April they bring with them an effervescent atmosphere of the rekindling of life after the barren days of winter. Like other summer visitors returning to the hills they will leave again during the first few weeks whenever the last vicious barbs of winter sweep back, but once they have returned for the summer they will not stay away long. The gulls bring a special flavour of life and activity with them because of their frequent density of numbers, their brilliant whiteness in the dark landscape of the hills, their incessant clamour in the colony and their constant traffickings to and from the lowland feeding grounds. Their first visits to the colony are cautious. They do not fly in immediately to reoccupy their ground, but the flocks circle at great height and only slowly approach and for the first few days will nervously erupt and fly at the slightest disturbance.

Once settled at the colony, activity is feverish as birds advertise themselves, establish pairs, defend territories and dispute with neighbours. Now the full purpose of the chocolate-brown head, common to both sexes, can be seen. Male birds determine their territories, the older, more experienced birds taking the favoured sites in the centre of the colony. On these territories they advertise themselves with special ritualized postures and poses, calling with long, rasping calls as they do so. Pairs mate for life and the established ones very quickly renew their bond; once the initial barriers of suspicion and caution are removed the reunited birds will display, not facing each other, as previously, in threat with bills pointed, but in similar posture side by side, breasts low and bills upturned. In all these poses, as in aggression to intruders, the brown mask is the prominent feature used at all times to exaggerate the movements and the stances.

Many of these hill colonies are small, merely a handful of pairs on a pocket-sized swamp, but others are large and contain many hundreds of pairs. In these colonies the clamour is ceaseless when the colony is occupied. Not only is each and every arrival greeted by a raucous stereotyped call from the partner, but disputes over territory boundaries break out continually. These are pugnacious and aggressive birds and physical contact is frequent, individuals – including chicks – being severely manhandled if they stray across an unseen boundary, although grievous bodily harm is rare.

NOISE AND AGGRESSION *vs.* **PREDATORS**

The gulls' main defence from enemies is through their strength in numbers and the massed protection which their noise and aggression bring. None the less predators will seek to profit from the multitude of chicks the gulls produce. Carrion crow, raven and short-eared owl are potential predators, and red kites will run the gauntlet of a furious swarm of angry gulls in an attempt to snatch a young one from the ground. Their low-level run through the colony is carefully timed and fast but their success rate is well below 100 per cent and they are frequently defeated by a mass of attacking gulls. In daytime the fox, too, is mobbed, his unseen passage across the hill traced for half a mile or more by a diving, screaming posse of flying gulls.

Snipe have become much scarcer, even in the hills, as land has been drained for agriculture.

Too soon these lively spring inhabitants of the river source will leave their hills, taking the year's new crop of tawny-winged young ones with them. By the time the holiday birdwatcher reaches the hill lakes the black-headed gulls have gone, their island slum left to be picked clean by the crows, later to be washed and spring-cleaned by the gales and rains of winter.

In other wet and spongy areas snipe breed too, although they can be unobtrusive and difficult to find for most of the day. In the evenings they appear, the male gracing the evening air with his plunging display flight, producing the rippling drumming sound with extended outer tail feathers as he plummets earthwards before peeling upwards to repeat the flight again. At other times he may sit, hunched and disconsolate-looking, on a splintered fence post; '*hic-cup, hic-cup, hic-cup*' he sings in a rhythmic, monotonous voice which wavers ventriloquially across the open hill.

DUNLIN, SECRET BREEDER ON THE WET HILLS

Dunlin too, tiniest of our breeding waders and scarce on most hills, visit these boggy sections of the hidden river in the evenings and the early morning to feed in the soft ground on a selection of larvae of craneflies, caddisflies, midges and the few beetles to which the soft mountain waters give rise.

Engaging and confiding birds, the dunlin come to these wet hills only in spring and summer, to breed in the safety and remoteness of the wide open spaces. At this time of year they are at their most attractive: the feathers of their upper parts show dark black-brown centres and are broadly edged with cinnamon to give an overall impression of bright chestnut. Underneath is a broad black patch on the belly and the flanks. The short, strong legs and the shining bill are all jet black.

Once on the nest in a tuft of rough grasses or short, sheep-grazed vegetation the incubating bird sits very tight and is difficult to find. The male does much of the incubating during the day and the female by night. In the warm

Scattered pairs of dunlin breed in the hills of southern Britain but are commoner in the north.

evenings of May the male indulges in his aerial display high above the breeding ground as he beats the bounds of his territory, flying in a wide circle and producing a thin, distant, whinnying trill. The sound catches on the mind and disappears; then it is there again, or is it? It has a strange quality of seeming distant and remote however close the bird is. This 'song' is not given to many birdwatchers to hear for they have usually left the hills by the time the evening dunlin flies, and it is only at the other end of the day in the early hours of the new morning that the dunlin will give away his presence, in the ecstatic diving flight of summer courtship.

On these high hills of Wales, northern England and Scotland the tiny dunlin are scarce and scattered breeding birds but although many areas where they formerly may have bred have been lost to afforestation and agricultural land improvement, dunlin have probably never been numerous. In winter, at the lower end of the rivers where they flood into the broad estuaries opening on the North Sea, Irish Sea and Atlantic, the dunlin renew their ties with the river; on almost all of the great estuaries of western Europe they occur in winter throngs with populations from Iceland, Scandinavia and Russia joining the smaller numbers of British birds. Dun-coloured birds then, without the chestnut spangling of summer and the black belly patch, they are one of the commonest and most familiar of estuary birds. Now on the high hills, however, they remain elusive and mysterious, the reward for the most diligent of river-source birdwatchers.

THE PLOVER'S PAGE

One of the dunlin's nicknames is the plover's page, a reference to its occasional habit of close association with the other bright and conspicuous breeding wader on the open hills, the golden plover. The strange and interesting relationship between them seems to occur at the instigation of the dunlin, a timid wader which benefits from associating with another who is vociferous and bold in withstanding aggressors. The association sometimes extends even to the merging of family groups feeding together on the hills before they depart for the low ground.

The golden plover in summer is the regal prince amongst the handful of birds which breed on the wet hills. A broad band of white, running all the way from forehead down to the flanks and the undertail, separates the jewelled black and gold of the upper parts from the jet black of face, throat and belly. It is sentinel too of these upland river bogs and heather banks. Nesting in the short, tight vegetation of the dry ridges, he commands a wide view and no one approaches him unseen. If the dunlin's nest is proof against predators through concealment and tight sitting, the golden plover relies on early warning. Constantly alert, it calls with the most melancholy and haunting of bell-like sounds long before a potential intruder – two-legged, four-legged or avian – is anywhere near the nest. The eggs themselves are cryptically coloured, merging tantalizingly with the broken pattern of mosses, lichens, peaty soil and heather stems in which the nest is formed.

None the less the dunlin's method is better, for many of the early nests of the plover are emptied by crow and fox. Where this happens, the pair may well be finished for the season even though they might be expected to re-lay if they lose their eggs this early. Often it seems that they are replaced at almost the same spot by a different pair making their attempt to breed.

By June most successful plover eggs will have hatched and the tiny young will be led away. Hatchling golden plover are the most exquisite of downy young. Minute, tail-less, black-and-golden – they are almost too improbably beautiful. They balance uncertainly on disproportionately heavy legs set well back on the body.

GOLDEN PLOVER CHICKS

Thus in the months of May and June, in the brief weeks of spring and early summer, the river's source pulses with bird life. This is the time to see the widest range of birds on the high watersheds, although even then bird-

watching will demand more patience and diligence than in most other situations. The heat of the day – the time by which most hill walkers have reached the depths of the hills – is in fact the poorest time to see birds which have their most intense activity in the hours soon after dawn and, to a lesser extent, in the fading light of evening.

The haunting, bell-like call of golden plover is one of the evocative sounds of the hills.

The greatest number of hopeful walkers make for the hills later in summer, in July and August, by which time many of the birds have gone and the watery hills and bogs are becoming silent again. At this season the gulls have left for the lowland river fields; dunlin, snipe and golden plover have also departed, the reed bunting is silent and the common sandpiper is no longer calling agitatedly on the lakeside. The hills are left to the red grouse, raven, wandering buzzard and crow and occasional hen harrier. Meadow pipits are still here though, ubiquitous and persistent, calling monotonously with beaks still crammed full of insects as they rear one brood after another.

YOUNG HERONS
VISIT THE HILL
POOLS

One other bird, the heron, fleetingly uses these lonely wet hills in late summer. At the end of the breeding season, from the heronries along the lower stretches of the rivers, the young herons wander away to fend for themselves, leaving the best feeding areas nearer the heronries as the favoured provinces of the adult birds. These young birds are inexperienced venturers, many of which will not make it through the first winter but will succumb to the cold and shortage of food if their lessons are not learned quickly during the bounty of summer and autumn. Those which come to the river's source are making an unpromising start. They will hunt for frogs or newts in the shallows of the pools, feed on the emerging craneflies in the wet bogs of the hidden river, and snap up any vole or fledgling pipit they might stumble on. This is a hard place for an apprentice heron to make its way, even in summer, and its time here is poorly spent. Just occasionally an adult heron

passes over the hill too, travelling from one river catchment to another on slow, bowed wings, with hunched neck and protruding feet. The grey heron, silent predator of marsh, lakeside, river bank and estuary, is the doyen of river birds, wedded to the river system from source to outflow. This is one species above all others which can be relied upon to accompany the long waters of the river throughout their course. Grey guardian of the river, a fisherman more practised and skilled than any other on the riverside, the heron's association with the river has a hundred thousand years of experience behind it.

As the waters of the hidden rivers gather and run off the slopes of the hill they come together in gathering streams, widening as each sparkling tributary joins. They cut their channels through the soft peat aeons ago and run fast over bare rock, tumbling in cataracts and falls as they pour down the steep scarps. Regular deluges of rain cause them to scour their channels and make it impossible for plants to find a secure foothold in the rocks.

BARREN STREAMS IN CONIFER FORESTS

Like many other upland rivers, the Severn soon flows into a dark shroud of all-encompassing conifer forest. As the streams speed through the forest cover, the trees crowd the side of watercourses and cut out the light. These are poor watersides for birds and only in the more open stretches are there occasional dippers or grey wagtails to brighten the dark forests of sitka. Also in these open areas, where old alders or birches remain beside the stream, siskins and redpolls may feed on the cones and buds in the bare twigs, but on the watercourse itself birds are few and far between; an insidious, unseen presence may well be at work. These mountain streams are legendary for their pure crystal water. This is easy enough to believe when one looks into the still waters of the rocky pools or the clear waters that pass over the gravel banks and bare bedrock. Traditionally the streams support good populations of trout, gudgeon and miller's thumb and have dippers and grey wagtails throughout their lengths. All of these feed on aquatic insects and thereby indicate the productivity and well-being of the mountain waters. All is not well, however, and the almost unnatural clarity of some of those waters is itself a clue to a fresh form of pollution through 'acid rain', which is now affecting upland water systems in Britain and on the Continent.

The two pollutants concerned, sulphur dioxide and nitrogen oxides, originate from gaseous emissions from power stations, factories, vehicles and so on. They fall, drifted by the wind either as dry deposition or in a wet form absorbed in rain and fog. When they fall they cause a slow acidification of the ground, especially where soils are thin (as in the uplands). This acidification can seriously affect the chain of wildlife in these areas as waters become slowly more acid and toxic metals such as aluminium are more readily released. In Scandinavia many lakes have already been rendered sterile; in Germany forest trees have been killed in wide areas and now in Wales the

Newly fledged herons – adventurers of the hills – hunt for food in upland pools.

ACID STREAMS,
REDUCING BIRD
NUMBERS

acidification of some lakes and streams has been proved to the extent of their having lost all fish stocks, much of their plant life and their invertebrates. Birds too must be affected in these circumstances, as has been shown in Sweden where ospreys and other water birds have vanished from lakes where they were once regular visitors. In Britain dippers, grey wagtails and common sandpipers will be the first to suffer on these upland streams but too little is known about their past populations to compare with their current status and show to what extent they have already been affected. The RSPB (Royal Society for the Protection of Birds) has done important work in the past few years in censussing the number of these and other species along entire river systems in Wales and dipper numbers, in particular, are being looked at carefully on a wide range of river sites where permanent monitoring points for checking acid levels are being established by the water authorities. Such work has important implications for the assessment of a problem such as this, but still it does nothing to mitigate it; in forthcoming years there could well be a marked reduction in the numbers of water birds in the upper reaches of many of our river systems. The problem is likely to be most acute in heavily afforested catchments as there appears to be a distinct link between the levels of acidification and conifer plantations. A perfect clue may be found on Plynlimon itself. Trout numbers have been carefully checked on the upper parts of the afforested Severn and the unafforested Wye, and it transpires that whereas the populations on the Wye are well up to the expected levels, those on the Severn are only a fraction of what they should be.

THE UPLAND RIVER

THE RIVER IN
ADOLESCENCE

*Tawny owls frequently
roost during the day in
the old riverside trees.*

The river has left the mountains now and a thousand streams from a thousand hillsides come together as growing rivers to plunge through the foothills towards the distant plains. These adolescent rivers are unruly and unpredictable: wild torrent sections, several miles in length, alternate with short placid stretches, tree-clad and rippled.

It is night and utterly still and silent. The last trace of day has gone and a misty crescent of autumn moon rises slowly across the eastern sky dimly lighting the distant plains of the river lowlands thirty miles down the valley. The river here is level and calm for a quarter of a mile, as if pausing briefly after one breakneck section to catch its breath before the next. On one bank it is lined with trees and on the other the little meadows, invisible in the dark, run bare to the water's edge. The moon filters through the silent branches of oak and alder to play weakly on the surface of the water with an eerie suggestion of lightness. Against the faint paleness of the sky the trees and the crowding hillsides stand in even blacker relief, spangled with the tiny distant squares of sharp light from small farmsteads dotted on the hillside.

A tawny owl calls a shrill '*keewik*' in the stillness; another, more distant, replies from across the valley. This is the autumn season when the owls must set up their winter hunting areas and dismiss the young to fend for themselves. '*Keewik*' is the call of the territory.

On the far side of the river where the edges of the grassy meadows lie right against the water, the moonlight catches the eddying current of a little stream that has wound its way through a wet marshy meadow and now joins the river. The only sound is the gentle pulling on meadow grass by the grazing sheep; against the lighter sky a leaf rattles softly against the twigs as it falls from an old alder and see-saws gently down, disappearing in the darkness and settling silent and unseen on the river surface to drift away. In the grey-blackness of the night all these are shadows now, but on the boggy spur where the two waters meet, on the very edge of the river one shadow shifts and moves away. Tall and slender, it has been still for a long time, but now its ghostly outline, barely discerned in the filtered moonlight, moves away from the river on to the marshy ground and faces the open meadow. With frightening suddenness, its long neck stretched forward, legs thrusting and great wings bowed, it launches into the air: '*FRAANK*' it calls, harsh and raucous, cracking the silence with spine-chilling force. The guardian grey heron has kept its river vigil well into the night and now heads for its safe tree-roost for what remains. Visible for a moment against the night sky, the heron swings towards the hillside and is lost once more in the darkness.

THE NOCTURNAL
HERON

There is very little that is random about the feeding habits of a bird like the grey heron. These are creatures of routine. Centred on the heronry (although they do not normally roost there outside the breeding season), adult

*Previous pages: the
upland river, well eroded
and fast-flowing,
abounds with birds.*

36

birds will range eight to ten miles from a colony to find their food and within this area they will know very well which are the best and most productive places to hunt. It is no accident that this night-time heron fished by the confluence of a little stream and the river. This is a favoured spot. In spring and summer the marshy field is bright with ragged robin, kingcups and yellow iris, and it regularly yields frogs, insects and small mammals; the shallow waters of the stream produce minnows and miller's thumb and there will usually be a heron here at some stage each day even if the visit is only brief. They concentrate their feeding at either end of the day, not infrequently going on into darkness if the need demands or if hunting is especially good.

SHEEP, CURLEWS AND THE UPLAND RIVER

This is the true upland river, descending rapidly from the mountains and passing through a countryside which is criss-crossed with a lattice of hedgerows, fences and small fields and studded with small farms built low on the hillsides. It is sheep country, and curlew country too: in winter the sheep are brought down to the shelter and accessibility of the enclosed fields, and in spring the curlews take over from them and nest in the long grass, bringing to these hills and valleys the most evocative of all sounds in upland areas.

The river has cut a deep valley by now which is revealed in rocky wooded outcrops and gorges in some stretches while otherwise the tapestry of small fields, neat hedgerows, copses and rough bracken banks clothes the valley on either side. Trees line the banks for much of the way – oak, ash, alder and sycamore. These are the last remnants, together with the hillside oak woods, of the woodlands which formerly filled the valley but have long since been cleared for the all-consuming interests of the sheep – patternmakers of the upland landscapes.

The broadening river is some seven yards wide now, but still the branches of oaks and alders arch together overhead to form a dark and leafy tunnel

Herons have their favourite and regular fishing spots, often used each day.

through which the water sparkles and sprays as it careers over the bare rock, cannoning off mossy boulders and stumbling over rocks. A bird, dark and dumpy with inadequate whirring wings, flies upstream inches above the cascading water. This is the home of the dipper, the only bird in the world in the vast order of passerines (perching birds) which has forsaken the land and learned to live a life which is totally dependent on the river. This is the one and only land bird which actually hunts its food under the water on the river's bed.

Green and mossy, the dippers' nest is always placed right by the side of the stream.

The dipper lands on a flat-topped boulder by the river's edge 50 yards away. It is difficult to see under the dark canopy of the trees but it moves and faces downstream again so that its bold white chest now shows clearly. The dipper is well named because as it stands there it bobs constantly, a metronome curtsey, its white nictitating membrane (or inner eyelid) flicking as it does so. The function of the rhythmic bobbing is an attempt, in conjunction with the white breast, to make the bird less visible against the background of dark rocks and broken white water. If this is the reason it sometimes seems to be one of evolution's lesser successes as it is frequently the very means by which the bird can best be located!

Dippers are the classic birds of these mountain streams where they run off the foothills and head for the flatter ground in the lowlands. On these torrent sections the dippers are truly at home and there are few rivers of this character on Dartmoor or Exmoor, in Wales, the Pennines, Peak District, Lakeland or most of Scotland which do not have good numbers of dippers. Birds of the hill areas of the north and west, they ignore the mellower streams of lowland England. Nor are they restricted to those sections of watercourses which are bordered by trees, for they can readily be found where there is very little cover, well up into the hills of the Pennines or Snowdonia. So long as there are exposed boulders, rocky sides, riffles or cataracts, the dippers can live happily in harness with the river. So wedded are they to the watercourses that it is amusing to watch them fly away when disturbed, faithfully following every curve of the river and never succumbing to the temptation to cut corners even where there are no trees or other impeding vegetation!

The dipper's total adaptation to underwater living is quite amazing. Almost all its feeding is done below the surface; it either walks in directly from the emergent boulders on which it perches, or plunges headlong into the stream waters, swimming strongly with the help of its wings. Underwater it walks around probing amongst the pebbles; it overcomes its natural buoyancy by holding half-opened wings at the appropriate angle so that the current presses the body down towards the bed of the stream. It flips over small stones to uncover the little nymphs of stoneflies and the larvae of mayflies which are their principal foods for most of the year. Indeed, it appears that the abund-

Dippers bobbing by the foam of a rushing torrent.

39

ance of these two insect families during the aquatic stages of their life cycles is the most important factor in determining the density and success of dippers. It is becoming increasingly clear that on many rivers, especially in afforested catchments, the growing acidification of the waters is causing the decline of these insects and consequently affecting the numbers of dippers which should occur there too. In these areas, sadly, dippers are already becoming more scarce.

DIPPER
TERRITORIES

Most dippers spend the whole year on the same stretches of river and have little cause to move away except from some of the highest reaches of the hill streams. Young birds remain close to their natal area but have to search for unoccupied territories where they can establish themselves. Like many other birds, dippers are territorial and defend their own stretches of river stoutly against intruders of their own kind who would compete, critically, for the precious supplies of food. Territory lengths are instinctively defined to ensure an adequate supply: where the rushing river is wide and boulders, riffles, gravel beds and rapids are numerous the territory will be short, perhaps as little as 400 yards, but where the stream is narrow the territory may need to be as much as a mile in length. The boundary of a dipper's territory – probably the longest and narrowest territory of any European bird – could not be easier to find. Follow the dipper along the stream and it will fly ahead of you each time until it reaches its territory limit, when it will turn and fly back past you; even this is a lesser fear for the bird than breaking and entering its neighbour's property!

Dippers nest early in the year, from mid-March on, and normally rear two broods. Their domed, mossy nest, skilfully sited out of the reach of spring inundations, is built under the arch of a bridge, on the open side of a waterfall or amongst the exposed roots of a riverside tree. The emerging youngsters abandon themselves to the water from the moment they first leave the nest.

In the shortening days of winter, before the turn of the year, the dippers are noisier than at any other time. They have a courtship song, tuneless, short and vehement, but arresting because of its passion and improbability. It is uttered either from their watery boulder perches or on the wing as they career high above the trees along the river, pouring out their unromantic song with the same energy and vigour with which they appear to carry out all their activities. This is the one time of the year when their flight path does not slavishly follow the watercourse.

No torrent seems too daunting for these robust little birds and they will happily hurl themselves into foaming waters, disappearing totally from view to reappear perhaps 30 yards downstream. They bounce to the surface like corks, then swim to the side and haul themselves out; the process is much repeated.

Few places are better for spotting dippers than the parapet of a bridge on the upland rivers; there you can just lean over and wait for the nearest pair to appear. These are also the places to find the colourful and delicate grey wagtails – so often partners with the dippers on the same stretches – and the two birds considered together are almost synonymous with fast-flowing, boulder-strewn streams. Their lifestyles are very different however.

There are only three wagtails – pied, grey and yellow – which normally occur in Britain. The pied (and its Continental equivalent, the white wagtail) is easy enough to identify, but people are easily confused by the other two. The grey wagtail does indeed show the bright lemon yellow of the underparts as its predominant colour compared with the pale slate grey of the upper parts. Its slender black tail is longer than any other wagtail's and it flicks it up and down ceaselessly as it moves along the water's edge or sits on streamside boulders. On the other hand the yellow wagtail, particularly the male, is an even brighter bird, canary yellow above and below. However, it lives in com-

THE THREE
BRITISH WAGTAILS

pletely different areas, being a summer visitor which principally inhabits lowland pastures and grazed marshes. The Continental race of yellow wagtails (blue-headed wagtail) also occurs sparingly in Britain, where it pairs readily with the indigenous all-yellow birds; the male has a blue-grey head and white eyestripe similar to those of the grey wagtail, but its other features and the different habitat should help to prevent confusion.

Grey wagtails are typical of the margins of the fast-moving hill streams.

One may be tempted to wonder why three members of the wagtail family – all riverside birds, all insect-eaters and all apparently similar in so many ways – should exist side by side. Could not one species of 'super-wagtail' take the place of all three? The answer lies in the fact that although the similarities among the three are real there are subtle but important differences in lifestyle that enable each species to occupy a markedly separate niche. For example, the yellow wagtail is a grassland feeder closely associated with lowland cattle pastures, particularly old meadows and grazing marshes. Its food supply is inaccessible in the British winter and therefore it migrates and spends that half of the year in Africa, south of the Sahara.

The pied wagtail is much more strongly associated with man's habitations and artefacts, being especially numerous around farms, sewage works and urban streams, and is not always to be found in direct proximity to water.

GREY WAGTAILS ON
THE WATERSIDE

The grey wagtail can be found in the fast-flowing upland sections of rivers. It is dainty, active and conspicuous, feeding on emerging waterside insects. It catches these by careful searching amongst pebbles in the little eddy-beaches behind rocky outcrops and boulders, through surface crevices on the mossy waterside rocks and, not least, sallying into the air in short dancing forays to catch the slow-flying adults of mayflies, caddisflies and midges on the wing.

Many of these upland grey wagtails retreat to the lowlands in winter to the more reliable winter feeding of sewage farms, lowland reservoirs, streams and watercress beds. Through spring and summer however they are the quintessence of life on these upland rivers: delicate and vivacious, they are the embodiment of the naiads – the spirit of the waters themselves.

FLOODING AND FLOOD PREVENTION

Floods in these upland stretches are rare. Rises in water levels may be truly dramatic and sudden but the rivers have steep gradients and have cut themselves deep channels quite capable of taking high flows without spilling out on to the adjoining land: the form of the valleys themselves, with steep sides and few flat areas, helps preclude such flooding too. Because of this the water authorities do not need to pay so much attention to these upland sections, so the mutilation of good wildlife areas that has occurred in the lowlands has been avoided. Water authorities, which have immense potential to determine the form and nature of Britain's rivers, have statutory responsibilities regarding both land drainage and flood prevention; frequently the work entailed causes bankside vegetation to be destroyed, and necessitates the removal of dead or overhanging riverside trees and the deepening of channels to ensure the uninterrupted dispersal of water down the river. This may be good for flood prevention but it is often disastrous for wildlife.

On the upland river such work is minimal; this factor, together with the rocky or marshy nature of much of the adjacent land (which so far defies serious agricultural reclamation), means that there are many belts of waterside trees or larger areas of woodland running alongside the river. Here, secure from chain-saw and plough, remnants of old woodland cling to the riverside banks and are a very precious wildlife resource in a rapidly changing countryside. Many of the woods are wet and boggy, dominated by alders and ashes. Others are on steep, dry slopes where oak predominate and ash, sycamore, wych elm and beech are scattered in amongst them. Important communities of birds are associated with both types. The birds have therefore become incidentally associated with the river, by accident of circumstance rather than design of nature. In an upland landscape which has otherwise been stripped of many of its woods and trees these linear corridors of woodland along the rivers and streams have come to assume considerable significance.

WOODCOCK IN THE WET HOLLOWS

Woodcock favour the wet alder hollows on the streamside in winter. Fed by seeping runnels of water from the rocky banks above, the ground remains boggy and open when hard frosts close over other damp areas. The woodcock probe here for earthworms and turn over the leaf litter for a variety of millipedes, earwigs, woodlice and beetles. They are secretive and strange birds, shrouded in mystery. As their name implies, it is usually in the woods that woodcock are found, amongst fairly thick cover. Most of their feeding is done after dusk when the birds leave the riverside woods, unseen, and fly 400–500

Marsh tits forage in the riverside woodlands.

yards to their favourite fields where they probe for earthworms under cover of darkness – when the worms tend to come to the surface. The birds will use the same field regularly, night after night, but by dawn are safely back in the shelter of the trees. They are well camouflaged against the wet blacks and browns of the woodland floor and have eyes set so far back on their heads that they are able to watch above and behind them for the threat of predators, even as they probe in the soft ground!

Secretive and mysterious, the woodcock is the bird of dusk, emerging only in the evenings.

WOODLAND BIRDS IN RIVERSIDE TREES

In the rotting stumps and dying limbs of old woodland trees great spotted woodpeckers excavate a harvest of hibernating insects and larvae. Marsh tits, tree-creepers and nuthatches are also common in such areas although there are winter days when the woodlands along the river seem eerily silent and quite devoid of birds. On another day the same patch can be alive. Foraging parties of siskins and redpolls, often in mixed flocks, love these riverside trees and both feed extensively on the seeds of silver birch and alders, as well as insects from the opening buds of larch in early spring. Both are acrobatic feeders, deftly turning and swinging on the thin outer twigs as they use their sharp bills to prise out the seeds. They have become very much riverside birds in winter, for nowadays this is where almost all the alders are to be found.

It is in the fullness of spring, however, that the real glory of these narrow woodland corridors is revealed. The ubiquitous hill sheep ensure that there is little or no undergrowth of brambles, nor much in the way of woody shrubs, but none the less the woodland floor is a rich green mosaic of mosses, ferns, woodland grasses and lichens. Patches of wood anemone and wood sorrel stud the ground and sheets of wild garlic and bluebells – both unpalatable to sheep – carpet parts of the wood. Amongst the welter of resident birds which return to the woods to breed in March and April – robin, blue-tit, great tit, rook, tawny owl, jackdaw and starling – there is an equal tide of long-distance

Summer arrivals add a great deal of sound and colour to the riverside woodlands.

summer visitors for which these waterside woods are especially notable. On this account these woods are especially popular with birdwatchers at this season.

COLOURFUL SUMMER VISITORS

Pied flycatchers come to breed in many upland valleys in Devon, Mid-Wales and the Lake District and are very common indeed in some areas. Bright and confiding, they are one of the delights of spring in the western half of Britain. They nest in smaller holes in old trees and will take to nest-boxes, if provided, more readily than almost any other species. Their nesting is timed to coincide with the huge harvest of defoliating caterpillars of oak tortrix, mottled umber and winter moths on the oak trees at the end of May and early June.

Redstarts, too, are common in riverside trees, also nesting in the safety of tree holes. The male is perhaps the most colourful of all summer visitors to the woods: grey back, orange breast, bold black bib, white forehead and a bright flash of rusty tail as he flies.

The most numerous warbler in these woods is the wood warbler, especially as the absence of undergrowth normally precludes the presence of more familiar garden warblers and blackcaps, which are more likely to be found in areas of rough bramble, gorse and hawthorn on the open parts of the river bank. The wood warbler spends much time in the canopy of the trees and has two distinctive songs. One is a liquid, melancholy note repeated fifteen or twenty times in quick succession and the other is an accelerating shivering trill, grasshopper-like in its climax, which the male frequently sings while moving about in the canopy.

Tree pipits and willow warblers like the open glades in these woodlands. The lesser spotted woodpecker, a resident bird rather than a summer visitor, has a predilection for nesting in alders where the soft wood allows it to dril'

out its nesting hole, often on the underside of a branch a few feet up over-hanging the river.

On these upland rivers the width of the valley varies from one place to another, and on some stretches it is two flat fields wide on either side. In such reaches the gradient is less steep and the form of the river is quite different. On one such stretch the Severn advances in two winding curves across the valley floor; three crescents of old alders and ashes close against the rising ground at the edge of the little plain mark earlier bends where the river once ran and cut its course against the flanks of the valley. This section is virtually bare of trees and has wire fences instead of old hedgelines – both sure signs of intensive 'improvement' made in the interests of agriculture once the valley floor becomes more level. Goosanders love this section and are frequently to be found fishing in the clear, deep stretches but they are wary birds and difficult to approach. Caution is needed if the birdwatcher is to get at all close to them, moving quickly whenever the birds are submerged, using what cover exists and being perfectly still again by the time they surface. It is a challenge, but well worth the time and effort, for these are unusual, colourful and exciting birds to see at close quarters.

THE WARY
GOOSANDER

On the outside of each curve the river continues its everlasting duel with the valley floor. It erodes at the base of the soft alluvial banks which have been deposited by the river's own floods over the centuries, and it carries away the spoil to the lowlands and, in the fullness of time, to the open estuary. Sand martins excavate their burrows in these soft, unstable banks, and in winter the river fills the holes and erodes the bank so that the season's work is lost.

On the inside of these curves, conversely, the river deposits its cargo of smooth and rounded shingles, hewn by waterpower from the rocks of Plynli-mon and smoothed by the transport of thirty miles or more. As the river cuts steadily into the alluvium-covered gravels on the far side of the channel the load of spreading shingle follows slowly behind it.

The gorse brakes on the shingle are rewarding places for several species.

THE SHIFTING RIVER

The farther one moves from the present channel of the watercourse the more vegetated is the shingle as time, and a gentle cover of fine silt, gives opportunity to the pioneering plants. The shingle is thus eventually disguised by a thin veneer of soil and left behind as the river inches farther across the valley. Although disguised, it lies too close to the surface to allow the encroaching plough. In this way broad sweeps of thinly covered shingle occupy the centre of the valley, criss-crossed here and there by false ox-bows into which the river spills first in times of flood. These hollows have a particular importance for birds because they are often muddy with deposited silt and many remain damp most of the year; they therefore become good feeding areas for insect-eating birds and for those which probe in the shallow mud for invertebrates.

Gorse dominates large parts of these flat, shingly areas. It is a successful pioneer and grows fast once it has gained a foothold in the shallow soils. It becomes an important agent itself in trapping silt and thereby accelerating the process of soil accretion. This will eventually result in its own downfall, for when the soil is deep enough the farmer will burn the gorse, put in the plough and sow new grasses to reclaim the area as pasture.

The riverside gorse brakes, sickly-sweet with heady fragrance in the fullness of summer, bring to the riverside several species of birds which would not otherwise be found here but for whom this is the only appropriate habitat in the region.

WHITETHROAT, STONECHAT AND BUNTING

Whitethroats come in summer to breed in the deep security of gorse and bramble thickets. They deliver a cheery, urgent song from the topmost spray of gorse or in dainty dancing song-flight. The stonechat, too, is typical of these areas, not only in summer but as a resident bird through the remainder of the year. Starting to nest as early as March, a pair will rear successive broods – sometimes still feeding a third brood up to the end of July. The male stonechat is particularly fine: black-headed and rusty-breasted, with a white neck patch, he cannot be confused with any other native bird. By June some of these gorse brakes are alive with young stonechat families, perching on the bushes and darting down to feed robin-like on the ground before flying up again.

Yellowhammers use these areas too, and where the first sallows or alders have established a toe-hold amongst the gorse or in the wet hollows reed bunting sometimes occur, overlapping with their near relatives in the same shingly areas.

Yellowhammers colonize the scrub areas which develop on the river shingle.

These gorse thickets are also of prime importance as lying-up places for otters. The classic river mammal of northern Europe, otters have been lost

Male Stonechat

Male Yellowhammer

Female Yellowhammer

Male Stonechat

Male Whitethroat

Female Whitethroat

Female Stonechat

Male Yellowhammer

from most of England now, but still occur in the south-west, in parts of Wales and substantially in Scotland. On the quiet, clean waters of the upper Severn in the (former) county of Montgomery the otter population is still significant. The creatures use these thick brakes, as they do on other river systems, to lie up in as an alternative to river-bank holts under the tangled roots of ash or sycamore.

Lapwings breed on the thin grasslands on the river shingles.

Lapwings nest on the open grassy areas of these shingles, away from the gorse, and in late summer and autumn flocks assemble to rest and feed before moving on to the coasts or to lowland winter areas on the richer agricultural land. Other wading birds use these shingles too at different times of year. Snipe feed in the wet hollows, and often in July or August passing green sandpipers or dunlin can be found here. The dunlin also use the water's edge; little parties of them – or sometimes single birds – probe the muddy patches amongst the shingle, chiefly for insects and their larvae.

RIVERSIDE WADERS
Whereas snipe and dunlin both use their long bills to probe in the soft river mud for their food, not all waders feed this way. Two other species which use these flat areas feed by pecking their food from the surface, searching amongst the pebbles on open parts of the shingle and on the mud and lightly vegetated patches. The first of these, the common sandpiper, breeds here, far downstream from the hill lakes where we first encountered it. The minimal nest is in a slight depression on the shingle, lightly camouflaged by the shadow of wispy grasses, or hidden amongst the litter of winter flood-wrack. By late summer those young birds which have been reared successfully feed alongside their parents in small family parties. Although the species is not gregarious, these family parties are often accompanied by other individuals, already passing south at the beginning of the long migration en route for west Africa and stopping off here on these flat riverside areas to feed. They fly from one side of the river to the other using a distinctive, peculiarly shallow, flicking wing beat, almost as though the bird flies too close to the water surface to permit a full downbeat.

The sandpipers are essentially northern and western in their breeding distribution and become scarcer in lowland England. This is the precise reverse of the distribution of the other, rather special, surface-feeding wader on these river gravels, the little ringed plover. Up to the time of the Second World War little ringed plovers were unknown as breeding birds in Britain and were exceedingly rare even as migrants. Since the 1940s they have not only gained a toe-hold but have subsequently achieved a very successful colonization of Britain. Their traditional breeding areas on the Continent are primarily river gravels but in Britain most of their breeding is associated with the post-war boom in lowland gravel-pits. On several river systems on the western edge of their expansion, such as Wye and Severn, where gravel-pits are scarce, the birds have resorted to their more typical habitats. This inland species must not be confused with its coastal relative, the ringed plover, which is slightly larger and more robust. In the inimitable way in which birds so often conspire to confuse us, the ringed plover too has started to nest inland over the past thirty years, probably due to the great human pressure on the coastal sand and shingle beaches where it preferentially nests. Inland nesting is particularly common in the north of England and Scotland, where it is not infrequent to find pairs nesting in exactly the same sorts of sites which are occupied by little ringed plovers further south.

OYSTERCATCHERS, INLAND BREEDERS

One other wading bird is associated with these flat upland river areas. The oystercatcher is probably the most familiar, and certainly the most easily recognized, of seashore waders. Its bold pied plumage and bright, orange-red bill are unmistakable and it draws further attention to itself through its noisy and excitable manner. Oystercatchers have shown a progressive tendency towards inland nesting during this century and they now nest in river valleys across northern England as well as fairly universally throughout Scotland and the islands. They not only nest on shingly banks and river islands but also widely in arable fields in the river valleys; and as if to demonstrate that they can move with the times (in a world where adaptability is as much a necessity as a virtue), they have been found nesting on stone walls, roof-tops, moorland and even in open woods! It is a far cry from the typical nest-site at the top of a shingle beach or on the grassy rocks on low sea cliffs. So, rather incongruously, the familiar seashore oystercatcher appears in these upland valleys to nest and to feed in the arable fields and even to follow the plough with the black-headed gulls. In doing this of course it forsakes its primary diet of marine molluscs for a summer menu of cranefly larvae, caterpillars and earthworms.

RIVERSIDE BIRDWATCHING

It can be seen therefore that these flat areas of river gravels have a whole variety of smaller habitats within them and that they are some of the best areas along rivers in which to see a wide range of bird species; in addition to those already mentioned wagtails, miscellaneous wildfowl, passage waders, seed-eating finches (goldfinch, linnet, greenfinch), corvids, gulls and heron are amongst the birds which regularly use these sites at different times of year. Waterside birdwatching is the easiest kind to enjoy – next in simplicity to back garden birdwatching from the kitchen window. This is partly because the most likely areas are easy to recognize, and partly because many of the birds, if approached stealthily, will be reluctant to leave the river itself and even if disturbed are likely to re-alight not far away. Carried out with reasonable quietness and caution any riverside walk can be rewarding for the bird-watcher. Perhaps the main lessons to learn are that bird-song and calls are as important as visual observation in locating and identifying birds and those

Little ringed plovers have colonized the river gravels in recent years.

who, like the anglers, are prepared to sit on the bank and wait for the birds to come to them will see most.

CORMORANTS, THE ANGLER'S ENEMY

Many river birds are viewed with admiration and affection but the cormorant is one species which has no claim to universal popularity. Although it is now fully protected under the Wildlife and Countryside Act the cormorant was, until 1981, the only river bird in England and Wales which was on the list of 'pest' species; it achieved this dubious honour because of its inland fishing excursions, not generally approved of by the angling community.

The cormorant is first and foremost an inshore fisher, living in shallow coastal waters and estuaries unlike the closely related shag (which it resembles but which is more marine in its habits and never uses freshwater). In Britain the cormorant is resident although birds disperse at random from the immediate areas of the breeding colonies at the end of the season. However the small population across the North Sea in Jutland and the southern coasts of the Baltic is necessarily a migratory one, with birds moving south-west to the Atlantic and North Sea coasts or crossing overland to the Mediterranean Sea for the winter.

COASTAL BREEDER, INLAND VISITOR

It is in autumn and winter that cormorants disperse from the breeding areas, and they are most likely to be found in the river valleys at this time. Prior to their persecution by fishermen during the past hundred years or so, they nested quite extensively inland (as many still do in eastern Europe), but now they rarely breed away from the coasts and are seen in the fresh upland waters mainly outside the breeding season. Their flight is powerful, direct and completely distinctive, with neck extended and a large, all-black silhouette.

They are common visitors on many sections of upland rivers. On the Severn, as it curves through the foothills, they regularly hunt the fish-rich waters and pillage the bounty of trout provided in the nearby reservoirs. They swim low in the water, sometimes half-submerged or with only neck and head above the surface as they wait to slip under the water to hunt. They give a distinctly reptilian impression, and in other ways and at other times these spectral birds have a somewhat uncomfortable and primaeval aura about them, their demeanour like that of a creature left behind from another age.

As the river unwinds from a long curve and straightens for the next quarter of a mile or so there stands the tall, bleached skeleton of a mighty elm, blasted and killed by lightning twenty years or more ago. Wind, storm and time have left it bereft of bark, small branches and twigs, and it stands now bare and upright, a solitary sentinel pointing only four blanched, wind-snapped branches to the sky. This is where the coven of cormorants gathers, their blackness stark against the pallor of the tree. They stand here gaunt in the winter air, sculptured, forbidding and ominous. On arrival each rests with

Cormorants perch, menacing and spectral, on the skeleton of an ancient riverside tree.

51

Goldeneye on the river: waterproofed and warm even in the iciest water.

wings outspread to dry; alone amongst winter birds they suffer the undeserved penalty of inadequate waterproofing.

Many of these river birds spend the majority of their lives actually in or on the water. Goosanders and grebes seldom come to land; tufted duck, pochard and goldeneye come ashore only for minimal periods and kingfisher, dipper and coot endure constant total immersions. The quality of waterproofing which these birds possess is so good that it is sometimes difficult for us to comprehend, especially when considered together with the fact that the birds' bodies must continuously be insulated against the cold to maintain a temperature of about 106 degrees fahrenheit (2 or 3 degrees lower at night).

On a bitter January day a goldeneye works to keep position in the middle of the deep, wind-chopped river channel. Thick ice fringes the river's edge and coats the bankside vegetation. Loose sheets have broken up from farther upstream and sweep past on the current; a searing Arctic wind whips across the river. A human life in these waters would not survive for eight minutes and yet the goldeneye, two pounds in weight and covered with three or four ounces of body feathers, dives unconcernedly to the river bottom again and again; he does the same each day and at night he stays there too, pulling into the quieter water out of the main current's flow.

WATERPROOFING AND TEMPERATURE REGULATION

Each day the goldeneye and all the other water birds must spend time maintaining and waterproofing their feathers. Those which seldom leave the water carry out their preening there too, drawing each flight feather gently through the bill and carefully working over the contour plumage. The preening is accompanied by much splashing, and by wing stretching as each feather is fitted into its proper place, the birds rolling on to their sides, often in a quite unrecognizable form, to groom the plumage of their underparts. The oily secretion from the preen gland at the base of the tail is meticulously applied to the feathers and keeps them waterproof, thereby preserving the life-giving insulation. Calm air is a poor conductor of heat, and the birds' feathers ensure the crucial insulation by stabilizing a layer of still, warm air in the down next to the skin. The dispersal of this layer of warmth by wind or movement of water is prevented by the tips of the contour feathers, which curve over the down and keep it in place. Underwater, the pressure of the water itself compresses the contour plumage to make this even more effective.

SAWBILL DUCKS

Two fish-eating ducks, the goosander and the red-breasted merganser, are typical of these fast-flowing upland rivers. Both are lean, rangy, long-necked ducks, streamlined for underwater pursuit. They belong to the family of sawbill ducks, so named because their bills are edged with backward-pointing serrations to facilitate the gripping of their fish prey. The family is unique in the whole world of wildfowl as the only one which pursues fast-moving prey under water.

The red-breasted merganser is characteristically a bird of estuarine waters and the lower sections of rivers. It is very familiar and numerous round the coasts of Scotland and northern England and has more recently spread as far south as Wales where, interestingly, it soon moved inland and now occurs in the upper sections of a number of the larger rivers, often alongside the goosander. On mainland Europe the merganser is predominantly Scandinavian and breeds only sporadically on the south side of the Baltic.

It has an unkempt, rangy appearance, exaggerated by a ragged, wispy crest and the wild crimson eye. The easiest places to see mergansers are certainly on estuaries and rocky coastal inlets where they are often numerous, especially in the north-west, Wales, western Ireland and western Scotland. In summer families of young often congregate together in the care of one or two 'nurse' adults and parties of thirty to fifty half-grown birds are not uncommon. On the upper reaches of these inland rivers the mergansers are shy and not easy to approach. Unlike mallard and teal, which often move into bank-side cover when approached before losing their nerve and flying, mergansers will fly at the first sign of disturbance.

THE HANDSOME GOOSANDER

The slightly larger and heavier goosander is a more typical inhabitant of the upland rivers, for among sawbills it is the freshwater specialist. It avoids weed-grown streams and prefers to hunt the clear waters of upland streams and lakes, where it pursues prey in the cold, fish-rich waters. Goosanders are extremely handsome birds. The males – appearing almost wholly white at a distance – are in fact black and white, with a dark green rounded head and narrow bright red bill. The white breast and underparts are subtly suffused with pink, visible in some lights and absent in others. The female, which is very similar to the duck merganser, has a crested chestnut head and is most reliably distinguished by the sharp line which divides this chestnut from the white of the breast.

Like several other species of duck (goldeneye, mandarin and sometimes mallard), goosanders are hole-nesters and are therefore restricted in the breeding season to areas which can provide old riverside trees with adequate holes for them to use. These holes, once used, will be regularly occupied even if they are fifteen feet or more above the ground. Nest-boxes have been readily taken where they have been provided in north-east England and Wales. In the absence of suitable trees the birds will sometimes find sites amongst boulders or rocks, and in Scandinavia they happily occupy the roof-space of riverside houses when they can find access under the eaves!

The Severn, fast and clear as it races off the foothills, is one of the rivers where goosanders have prospered in recent years. Here they sight-hunt trout, young salmon, grayling and miller's thumb in the clear waters, either pursuing them in the shallows, swimming with head and neck underwater, or diving in the deeper pools to chase them with strong thrusts of their legs. Most of the

fish they catch are less than four inches in length but the preference which they seem to have for salmonids has brought them into conflict with anglers in certain parts of the country and they are heavily persecuted in some areas.

Goosanders are not primarily bottom-feeders but will happily use their thin, pointed bills to probe round stones to dislodge fish hiding beneath. Often, too, pairs or small groups hunt together (mergansers also do this), searching the waters with head and eyes submerged and driving the fish ahead of them in line abreast.

NEST-BOXES FOR DUCKS

Near the Severn there is a nest-box, put up for tawny owls on the branch of a tall oak standing beside the footpath along the water's edge, which the goosander have taken as their own and claimed as an annual nest-site. The tiny ducklings, eight to ten of them each year all hatching on the same day, bale out of the nest-box within hours of hatching and drop, puny legs stretched below them and futile featherless wings extended, unharmed on to the hard foothpath fifteen feet below. Nearby at the base of the great Clywedog reservoir each June a female goosander who nests on the stream below the dam manages to get her entire brood trapped. She guides her half-grown brood upstream towards the reservoir and inevitably ends up with the whole brood hopelessly imprisoned within the vertical concrete walls of the stilling basin. In some years they have been preyed upon by carrion crows as she attempts the impossible task of leading them up the face of the dam to the deep, fertile fishing waters above. Each year, too, the sympathetic Severn-Trent Water Authority staff conscientiously drain the stilling pool, pursue the unbelievably fast-moving baby ducklings over the treacherous base of the concrete basins, catch them and put them safely on the reservoir waters above.

Creatures which are otherwise terrestrial need certain adaptations to be able to feed underwater, for there may be particular problems of locomotion, vision, countering natural buoyancy and (for some) locating and capturing mobile prey.

ADAPTATIONS FOR UNDERWATER SWIMMING

Underwater fishers need special adaptations of sight to enable them to locate prey before chasing it. How is it that a bird such as the goosander or the grebe, in pursuit of fast-moving prey such as trout or salmon parr, can locate it, focus and estimate distance while moving through the water itself? The answer is that underwater the goosander searches with its head moving in a series of jerky movements. The back stroke of the legs is accompanied by a stretching of the neck and as the legs are drawn forward again the neck is withdrawn too. By this means the eyes are moved through a series of fixed positions in relation to the bed of the river and other three-dimensional objects instead of having to cope with the moving blur which would result if the head and body moved forward continuously in unison. This neat device is

Tree holes are the most usual riverside site chosen by goosanders for nesting.

Red-breasted mergansers are estuary birds which have spread into many inland rivers.

dispensed with once prey is located and pursuit is under way. Then there is no longer the need for visual acuity: instead, speed is of the essence and with neck fully extended the goosander becomes streamlined and dart-like to maximize the chances of capture.

DIFFERENT
SPECIES'
ADAPTATIONS

The 'third eyelid' or nictitating membrane is an important mechanism for many birds and has special functions for underwater swimmers. This membrane lies under the eyelids on the nasal side and is drawn horizontally across the eye to protect it. Important though this is, it has the potential disadvantage of obscuring sharp sight underwater. The solution is simple! The goosander and many other diving birds have a nictitating membrane with a clear lens-like panel in the centre. This is so highly refractive that it will bend light rays, thus helping to compensate for the loss of refraction from the cornea of the eye itself.

The dipper's remarkable ability to walk on the river-bed, mentioned earlier, is one of several equally neat adaptations found in river birds. For example, grebes feed substantially on fish, which requires skill and speed, so in order to enhance their streamlining the flight feathers are curved towards their outer ends so that when folded to the body – as when underwater – they are actually tucked under the contour plumage. The hind toe of a diving duck, such as a pochard, has a small flattened lobe on it (absent on the dabbling ducks because they have no need of it) which helps to give the bird 'fine tuning' for underwater manoeuvres.

Legs and feet are the exclusive methods of propulsion for all river birds which dive for their food (some sea birds such as penguins and auks use wings and actually 'fly' underwater) and so many of them have strong thick legs and webbed feet to act as paddles. Coots are members of the rail family and the only British representative which habitually feeds underwater. None of the family therefore has webbed feet, but the coot has developed widely lobed toes which operate similarly to webs, producing a wide surface area with which to thrust against the water. A coot's pelvis and hind limbs are also adapted from the normal arrangement in other members of its family to improve its diving ability.

Although steering underwater is achieved mainly by the asymmetrical use of the feet, some hot-pursuit birds, including goosander, merganser and cormorant, possess longer tails than other diving water birds for whom fast mobility is of less importance than the need for an independent rudder.

THE LOWLAND RIVER

The river's pace has slackened. Never again will it regain the power and urgency of its exit from the hills. Now that it is mature it has exchanged urgency and power for a quieter internal surge. It has changed colour too, as other silt-laden rivers have joined it to carry their precious load of soils downstream to replenish the lowland fields and the far-distant estuary.

The valley, previously so sharply defined between the hills, has disappeared too, and the deep brown river curves in a serpentine course across the plains. The cloak of oaks, ashes, bracken banks and small sheep meadows through which it passed has now been replaced by a different type of countryside. Flat and fertile, most of it is intensively farmed with broad, arable fields spreading across the river's alluvial plain on either side. On the bank and along the field edges are tall willows, their roots flourishing in the waterlogged earth which other trees shun. On this slower, winding river dipper and grey wagtail, goosander and sandpiper are now replaced by sand martin, reed bunting, sedge warbler and moorhen.

THE RIVER IN MATURITY

The Severn is one of these swelling rivers. It has left the broken hill country of the Welsh Marches to be joined by its tributary, the Vyrnwy, on the English border. The land is completely flat here for a mile or more either side, for in a former age this was one huge post-glacial lake fed by the waters of these two mountain rivers. Long since choked, silted up and made firm by the passage of time, the area is now a quiet rural backwater across which the rivers wind their lazy way. It has the comfortable, friendly feeling of a familiar English landscape that is now lost; a corner forgotten by time, protected from change by the river itself.

WETLAND LANDSCAPE

The land is so low and the volume of winter floodwater so great that it is impractical to drain the whole area; to do so by constraining the floodwater within the channel would merely exacerbate the problem of flooding further downstream. Therefore the confluence area becomes an essential system of washlands over which the river spills in winter and then releases the waters gradually, thus alleviating flooding lower down. It remains a patchwork of odd-shaped, odd-sized fields bounded by old, unkempt hedgerows and punctuated with ancient oaks and elms. As all these old trees provide abundant nest-sites this is a fine area for barn owls, kestrels and stock doves, amongst others. The doves are particularly common, although easily overlooked amid the greater numbers of woodpigeons. They are beautifully plumaged birds, darker blue-grey than the woodpigeon, with bright, wine-coloured breasts and iridescent green patches on the sides of the neck. They like to feed behind the receding floods where the waters have released seeds hidden in the vegetation or have freshened the leaves of clover on which the birds feed.

On the edges of the flooded meadows stock doves find rich feeding.

60

There are little owls here, too; they nest in the plethora of holes in the old trees and hunt the hedgerows at dusk and in the early mornings for beetles, small birds, mammals and other small prey. They do especially well when the waters are high and the prey is concentrated on the higher ground on the ditch banks.

The little owl, a nineteenth-century introduction from Europe, is now a well-established British resident.

In many fields wet hollows occur which are fringed with pollards or draped with ancient shattered willows, split by the ravages of storms and by their own spreading weight. Elsewhere shallow flashes appear as soon as heavy rains fall, mapping the pattern of former river courses and marshes. In the modern ditches and channels which criss-cross the body of the erstwhile lake bulrush, reed, reed sweet-grass and pondweeds still indicate the former nature of the land. In some of the hollows osiers grow, which in summer provide homes for noisy pairs of sedge warblers and ring with the persistent, artless song of reed buntings.

In winter the wet fields, flashes and pools attract a wide variety of wild-fowl, drawn by the rich grazing and the secure roosting sites. Some flocks roost at night on the open floodwater, where they are safe from patrolling foxes, while others habitually use the river or resort to it at times when other standing water is scarce.

WILD SWANS

With luck, all three species of wild swan can be found here: Bewick's, whooper and mute. British mute swans have no need to migrate because, generally speaking, their feeding areas remain unfrozen throughout the year. They breed on the islands and in the reedy backwaters of the river. After the young hatch, in June, it is another four months before they are able to fly. Once the cygnets are on the wing, however, in late autumn and early winter, the local population from this part of the valley usually congregates on the wet fields, tending to remain together until the adult pairs move off once more to

Whooper swan

Male
mute swan
aggression
display

Female
mute swan

Immature
mute swan

Whooper and
bewick's
swans →
←

Juvenile mute (top).
and whooper swans

the breeding sites in March and April. The winter flock of thirty or more spends much of its time grazing on pastures and on winter cereal crops – a seasonal alternative to the mute swan's staple summer diet of aquatic plants. During the months when they are on the waterside, nesting or accompanying their broods, water plants are obviously the most readily available foods.

On a dark autumn day Bewick's swans arrive for the winter.

BEWICK'S SWANS

Bewick's swans pass through and sometimes linger en route for wintering grounds in Ireland. They are the long-distance migrants amongst European swans, breeding deep in the Siberian tundras east of the Taymyr river and wintering in the ice-free zone of north-west Europe, mainly in Britain, Holland and Denmark, and to a lesser extent in West Germany. Their breeding must be brisk and businesslike. There is no luxury of four-month fledging for the young Bewick's swans. Breeding starts for this tundra swan even before the summer thaw is fully under way and the whole cycle from egg-laying to the young flying must be rushed into a maximum of 130 days. Incubation is a whole week shorter than for the mute swan and the fledging of young takes no more than 45 days – one-third of the time of the young mutes! By early October the breeding grounds have been abandoned and the birds are en route by easy stages to the relative mildness of western Europe. Breeding in the harsh environment of the high Arctic is hazardous, even with the bounty of food which the brief summer brings. Often the swans breed with only minimal success; sometimes they fail completely. Adult birds pair for life and the families stay together for the winter, enabling the varying fortunes of each breeding season to be easily followed, revealed by the number of young accompanying the parents. Many pairs arrive with no young, but Bewicks are long-lived birds and statistically they need to produce only two successful young throughout their lifetime to maintain the population.

The moment of the arrival of the wild swans can be exciting – both for the birds and for any birdwatcher whose good fortune it is to witness it. Once, on a rough, overcast day in late October near one of the open-water flashes, four swans approached flying steadily from the east. Their whiteness was vivid against the dark sky and the naked trees as they swung in towards the water. It was evident that they knew their destination well and were thoroughly familiar with the surroundings. Without hesitation and almost in line abreast they swept low over the line of pollard willows and straight towards the flash; with legs pressed forward and webbed feet spread, their great wings braced as air brakes and their necks extended for balance, they planed majestically across the surface and came to a halt. How far they had come in that one flight only they could know but their sense of achievement was evident: they knew exactly where they had been heading and they had now arrived. They called triumphantly, heads held aloft, and displayed feverishly with much wing-stretching, head-bobbing, shaking and chasing. Their behaviour seemed to

Whooper, mute and Bewick's swans frequent the flooded water meadows.

Wigeon and teal are winter wildfowl of the lowlands.

be an avian interpretation of the human expressions of excitement and relief, but within a minute they were composed and dignified again, adjusting their plumage with gentle movements and starting to feed in the shallow water.

ICELANDIC WHOOPERS AND NORTHERN GEESE

If Bewick's swans travel from the distant east, whoopers have a similar but much shorter journey from the north-west, travelling across the North Atlantic from breeding grounds in Iceland. They too are grazers, up-ending to feed on the roots and stems of aquatic vegetation such as pondweeds, crowfoot, reed grass and horsetail. In recent years they have shown a growing tendency to frequent farmland, where they graze winter cereals, stubble, spilled potatoes and other roots. Sometimes one or two of these wintering whoopers stay on in Britain, perhaps when a bird has been pricked by shot, or otherwise injured, and there have been several records of breeding attempts, especially in Scotland.

Wild geese turn up on these fields in most years but there are never many and their frequency and numbers vary depending on both weather and ground conditions. Greylags, pinkfeet and European whitefronts are the most regular; small parties sometimes turn up unexpectedly to graze warily in the largest wide-open fields for a few days, but they soon disappear again.

The wet fields are ideal for dabbling duck, and packs of wigeon, teal and mallard are present throughout the winter months. This concentration of birds attracts avian predators, too: peregrine winter here, terrorizing the packs of duck and flocks of waders; merlin and sparrowhawk pursue the thrushes and finches, and occasional hen harriers quarter the rough areas and wide banks of the ditches. Throughout the course of one winter more than twenty different species of waterbirds will use the area, in addition to nine or ten wading birds and miscellaneous others. In January 1984 when Scotland and Northern England were blanketed in deep snow the whole of this wet plain was alive with thousand upon thousand of fieldfares and redwings – and lapwings, too – escaping from the frozen grounds further north to find open feeding in the Severn lowlands.

THE MAJOR
WASHLANDS

Washlands such as these are crucial inland wintering areas for birds but since the Second World War huge areas have been lost, through drainage, to the insatiable demands of agriculture. Today the important areas remaining are few. They are widely scattered and many of them are under severe continuing pressure – Derwent Ings in Yorkshire, the Somerset levels, the Yare marshes in Norfolk and the Pevensey levels in Sussex. Each time one of these areas is lost or reduced the others assume an even greater importance.

The washlands on the Severn-Vyrnwy confluence are interesting and of some regional importance but they are small fry compared to the really big washlands in East Anglia, the water meadows on the great fenland rivers Ouse and Nene. This is where the Dutchman Vermuyden carried out huge drainage schemes in the seventeenth century, one of which was the canalizing of 21 miles of the Great Ouse river in Cambridgeshire, eventually enclosing it between two parallel flood channels half a mile apart. The banks of the two channels serve to contain the floodwaters of the Ouse as one enormous long, narrow lake in times of flood.

The area is of international importance for its winter wildfowl and nationally important for breeding birds. The RSPB and other conservation bodies already own over 2,000 acres of this site, so much of it is now permanently safeguarded; furthermore, it provides unparalleled opportunities for the public to see the birds in great numbers and at close quarters.

Here the sheer numbers of wintering birds sometimes defy imagination. Thirty thousand wigeon are regularly present, with peak counts rising to as many as 40,000. Almost half the population of Bewick's swans wintering in

Greylag geese graze in the wet meadows.

western Europe are found here, having gradually increased over the past fifteen years to more than 3,000 individuals. There may be over 4,000 teal present throughout the washes at any one time, 2,000 mallard, 1,000 pintail and 500 shoveler; tufted duck, gadwall, pochard, shelduck and mute swan are also counted in hundreds.

RARE BLACK-TAILED GODWIT AND RUFF

On these washes there is a traditional pattern of winter flooding/summer grazing/haymaking. The land is too wet to be ploughed for cereals and old management regimes are therefore retained. In summer the fields, ditches and banks are ablaze with yellow flag, loosestrife, comfrey, buttercups and white umbellifers, home for a host of breeding birds. It was to these Ouse washes in 1952 that the tall and graceful black-tailed godwit returned to nest, having been absent from Britain as a regular breeding bird since the early part of the last century. Since 1952 it has slowly increased its numbers to between forty and sixty pairs nesting here in any one year. This slender, long-billed wader nests amongst the rank grasses of the water meadows and has a beautiful and evocative courtship display. The male rises in steep flight with rapidly beating wings calling repeatedly 'wikka, wikka, wikka'; it follows the steep climb with sudden tumbling aerobatics and dives, often vertically, with wings folded back to within a few feet of the ground.

Most exotic of British waders, the rare and beautiful ruff also returned as a breeding species in the 1960s and is securely established now, though not as numerous as the godwit. At the onset of the breeding season the ruffs congregate at ritual lekking sites where the males perform frantic scuttling displays with their amazing ruffs extended and wings spread. The females (reeves) attend the leks, thereby galvanizing the males into frenzied fencing action; it is the reeves who select the mating partner. The male plumages are extremely variable, hardly any two being exactly the same. The strange neck feathers, ranging from white through buff, chestnut and purple to black, may be either plain or barred, but they are produced quickly and retained only during the brief period of courtship during late April and May.

The summer water meadows are full of other breeding waders too, notably lapwing, redshank and snipe, all of which are very numerous in the Ouse washes. Wildfowl nest here in wider variety than on most other British sites. Mallard apart, the numbers of duck breeding in the British Isles are modest by most standards but here on the gem of all British river-meadow sites shoveler, shelduck, gadwall, teal, garganey, tufted duck and pochard all nest in the rough pastures and banks and on the new islands and ditches being created by the RSPB. In June the washes are at their zenith. The meadows and the wide ditches pulsate with new life: the inexhaustible goodness of the river quickens the wildlife of the lowlands.

Breeding waders are numerous here but it is salutary that a bird such as the common snipe – the archetypal breeding species of wet meadows – should have been gradually reduced over southern Britain through the drainage of other riverside water meadows. Estimates of the British population in 1972 suggested in excess of 29,000 pairs breeding in the lowlands; however, in 1983 the RSPB showed that there were probably only 5,000–10,000 throughout England and Wales.

COMMON SNIPE

The common snipe that fills the summer evenings along the riverside with its buzzing song flight or springs out of rushy hollows in winter will become an increasingly rare sight.

The opaque depths of the lowland river are brown and turgid – a far cry from the crystal waters of the fast-flowing upland river. Despite its colour and the strength of its inner momentum there is now a maturing serenity about the river; gone are the noisy, conversational chatter of the mountain stream and the cascading torrents of the uplands. The river moves now in an eerie silence, swirling down the centre of its channel with quicksilver ripples racing

Spectacular ruffs and godwits – rare birds of the summer washlands.

Black-tailed
godwit
(summer)

Black-tailed
godwit
(summer)

Ruff
(winter)

Reeve (summer)

Ruffs
at lek

displaying
endless variation
in their nuptial plumes

hither and thither ahead of the current. At the sides of the channel the waters eddy and swirl, some moving slowly back upstream for many yards before becoming caught in the current and swept onwards again. The river pulls at the trailing fronds of overhanging willow branches and tugs at the clumps of sapling wands growing from the waters themselves; the wands bend slowly downstream in unison until nearly flat on the water and then spring back, metronome-like, so that momentarily the water rushes noisily through them – the only sound of the wide river.

In late winter the trembling willows are a glowing, lustrous ochre in the low afternoon light. The dry, broken stalks of last year's nettles, reeds and willow herb on the bank are starkly white against the flood-washed green of the pastures and the mirror reflections of the dark trees in the stranded pools of flood water. A moorhen calls unseen from the slack brown water among the osiers by the bank. The river landscape, a rich tapestry of winter colours, is the lifeblood of the lowlands and the focus, too, for the urban angler.

It is calculated that there are some 3,500,000 anglers in Britain; a high proportion of these are coarse fishermen, mainly radiating outwards from the urban areas, who use the river banks intensively for much of the year. The close season for coarse fishing extends from 14 March to 16 June because this is the main breeding season for the fish themselves, but by chance it fits in conveniently with the interests of other river wildlife: bankside vegetation, growing fast in April and May, has the chance to recover from winter trampling and will thereafter provide reasonable sanctuary for birds nesting in its cover. This sleeve of rank waterside vegetation on either side of the river is of paramount importance in enabling a variety of bird species to colonize the lowland river.

On many sections of lowland rivers where there is rank vegetation or rough scrub, sedge warblers are plentiful. They are typically seen where there is luxuriant waterside growth but are equally happy – perhaps more so – in drier thickets of scrub with hawthorns and tangled brambles or osiers. Their nests are well hidden and difficult to find, placed low down in very thick cover. Sedge warblers are successful birds with a very wide distribution, reflecting the abundance of suitable habitat available to them. Primarily, however, they are birds of the lowland river valleys.

They have a conspicuous song flight in which the male bird rises perpendicularly from its perch and then descends rapidly to the same branch or to an adjacent one. The song is just as frequently delivered from the song post. Strident and far-carrying, it comprises a hurried medley of repeated phrases. The bird is a skilled mimic, too, and careful listening makes it possible to identify snatches of song from swallow, blackbird, starling, whitethroat, skylark and other birds.

THE CHARACTER OF THE LOWLAND RIVER

RIVERSIDE BUSHES AND SEDGE WARBLERS

Resident birds, as well as summer visitors such as the sedge warbler and whitethroat, are certainly plentiful along many of these lowland sections. Many of these birds are not here because of the river itself but because the banks are lined with old trees and have rough brakes of blackthorn, hawthorn, bramble and other scrub. Robins, dunnocks and wrens are therefore as numerous along the banks of many lowland rivers as they are on farmland or in woodland; blackbirds and song thrushes too find secure nesting sites in the bramble thickets swathing the bases of riverside trees. Many of the old oaks and elms are ivy-covered and not only offer nest-sites for the thrushes and greenfinches, wrens and robins but also provide a harvest of berries in the depths of winter for woodpigeons, blackbirds and other residents. These riverside trees are popular with nuthatches, treecreepers and both great spotted and lesser spotted woodpeckers. The treecreeper's delicate curved bill is ideally suited to probing the deep crevices of bark while the woodpeckers, equipped with powerful bills, reinforced skulls and abnormally long tongues can chisel away the dead branches and extract insect larvae from their tunnels deep inside the wood. In summer spotted flycatchers, blackcaps and garden warblers, nightingales and turtle doves join the throng of birds along the lowland rivers and confirm them to be some of the best and most rewarding places for the birdwatcher.

WILD DUCK AND WATERHEN

Mallard favour the quiet stretches of the river, and when danger threatens or the quiet of the riverbank is disturbed they will draw in under cover and wait until all is clear again unless the threat becomes too alarming and they are forced to take wing. Moorhens also use riverside cover for sanctuary and will often nest in the tangles of overhanging vegetation, which provides greater safety for them than the vulnerable nests they otherwise build in rushes at the water's edge, where both rising waters and avian predators may encroach.

A pair of mallard – wild duck – with bankside irises on the lowland river.

MOORHENS,
FAMILIAR BUT
ENIGMATIC

Moorhens, very familiar birds on farm ponds, canals, town lakes and similar still waters, also make use of quiet stretches of slow-moving rivers. On some sections of the Severn, for example, there are as many as five pairs per mile. (It is postulated that the national population for this abundant waterbird exceeds 300,000 pairs.) Despite being so common and familiar the moorhen rarely attracts much attention, which is a pity because it is interesting and unusual – indeed, surprising – in several respects.

Its appearance and its habits are very well known, but many people's knowledge of the bird stops there. Moorhens are readily recognized by their jerky swimming action, bright red bills and red frontal shields. Their white flicking under-tail, signalling its warning, is conspicuous; so too is their habit of pattering across the water when disturbed, flying the last few yards with legs trailing.

These common river birds are members of the world-wide family of rails (the other two British residents are coot and water rail) and are equally at home on land and on water: they spend much time on the water but in fact their large feet with long, thin toes – typical of many of the wetland members of the family – are better suited for dry land and marshes than for aquatic life, as they are inefficient, unwebbed paddles. Despite this, moorhens are good climbers and many pairs nest in bushes and trees on the bankside rather than down at water level. They also roost in similar sites out of reach of ground predators. Their night life is somewhat strange and little understood because in addition to feeding occasionally when there is strong moonlight, they are quite vocal, especially in spring and autumn; for reasons still best known to themselves they often fly round at night calling with a low, gutteral grunt.

They are aggressive birds to others of their kind during the breeding season; where pairs are in close proximity skirmishing is frequent and charg-

ing attacks across the water with wings and legs beating are commonplace. The bold red frontal shield is important in these encounters and is lowered and presented towards the adversary as the first stage of hostility. At the end of the breeding season groups of varying size, usually between 15 and 30 individuals, will form loose wintering flocks. Within these there is a distinct social pecking order. This hierarchy, in which the biggest and strongest are most successful, is determined not strictly by the strength or aggression of individual birds, but the size – and hence prominence – of the red shields; for this reason the older males, and after them the females, tend to be dominant over the other members of the group.

Moorhens are numerous on quiet sections of most lowland rivers.

ADAPTATION TO THE MODERN WORLD

When a bird species does as well in the modern world as the moorhen has done, we can be sure that it has adapted well to man, shown itself to be capable of breeding fast and successfully and ensured itself access to an ample food supply through the year. The moorhen meets all these requirements. It is an omnivorous feeder, happily existing on a wide range of animal and vegetable foods, and can readily find these in very close proximity to human habitation, notably in urban areas. It is a prolific breeder, starting early in the year and producing two or even three successive broods, from 6–8 eggs each time. Losses of first clutches are often high (50 per cent or more) when riverside cover is poorly developed, but the success rate increases as cover thickens through the season; the black, downy chicks with garish red bills and faces are second only to coots in sheer ugliness. Juveniles from the first brood are fed by the parents up to about six weeks of age but will later take an active part in family life by helping the brooding and feeding of young birds from later broods.

The river in summer is not only quickened by the movement and activity of birds but is alive also with their sound. To identify the different calls and songs is to realize just how many birds are there, unseen, at any given time.

'*Cheee, cheee.*' A shrill, piercing whistle drifts across the river. A few moments later it comes again from further round the bend, its perpetrator still unseen. This is one of the sounds of the lowland river: a sound from a bird which is more frequently heard than seen, despite its brilliant colours. For this is kingfisher territory and the shrill whistle is the first manifestation of its presence, because despite its brightness it is not always easy to pick out against the welter of summer colours on the river bank. Not that the king-fisher has always been so brightly coloured, if we are to believe the beautiful old French legend quoted by David Boag in his book *The Kingfisher*. When Noah became impatient for the return of the dove and could wait no longer, he released the kingfisher to search for signs of land because its large beak showed it to be courageous and as a fisherman it was not afraid of the waters of the Flood. As the grey-plumaged kingfisher flew high to avoid a storm it was struck by a bolt of lightning which left a strip of brilliant electric blue down its back from head to tail. Flying higher it felt the warmth of the sun but came too close and scorched first its chest, then, as it turned away, its tail too. By the time the kingfisher eventually returned to earth the Flood had g and the ark had been dismantled. Ever since, the kingfisher has ceaseles travelled the rivers calling and searching for its old master.

Kingfishers are highly territorial birds, aggressive to other individuals throughout most of their lives. It is important that they maintain an exclusive territory to assure sufficient food supply through the difficult months of winter. Also when a pair is united in the breeding season it must be sure that it can catch ample food on which to feed the young of successive broods without struggling with competition or having to travel wasteful distances to find it.

On lowland rivers like the Thames, Ouse, Trent or Avon kingfisher territories vary somewhat in length, depending on fishing conditions, but are generally a mile or so long. A kingfisher knows its territory intimately, in much the same way as we know the exact details of the home, garden and street in which we live. Its world is defined by an invisible but totally rigid boundary beyond which it will not move unless something totally untoward occurs. The territory will have several essential features – a choice of favourite and productive fishing spots, adequate bankside perches, a sheltered roost-site, and soft earth banks that can be tunnelled for nesting. Side streams flowing into these sluggish lowland rivers are especially desirable as they provide additional shallow water for fishing. Small ponds and clear ditches further away from the river will add to the value of the property and be stoutly defended even if they are only used in emergency.

In the shared world of the breeding season when food is plentiful, the

Two kingfishers plunge in clear water to capture minnows.

The brilliant kingfisher – a flash of colour – is a resident on most lowland rivers.

young of the first broods are tolerated in the territory while second broods are being reared. Once September arrives, however, the young are no longer welcome and are unceremoniously chased from the territory; the adult birds themselves also split up and set up separate bases. One of them may retain all of the territory or alternatively it will, in good divorce fashion, be divided between them for the autumn and winter. Sometimes an uncomfortable area of shared ownership may occur, perhaps where both are reluctant to give up a particularly rewarding fishing spot; in this tense situation each bird will approach nervously and much competitive sparring will take place.

The high-pitched, strident whistle, sometimes single, frequently double, is used by the kingfisher as an advertisement of territory ownership. It is issued with confidence and panache, particularly as a bird approaches a regular perch signalling a warning to any intruding kingfisher. In late summer young kingfishers start to employ territory calls too, but once they are in the process of being ejected from the natal stretch they may craftily stop using them, in order to continue visiting a favourite fishing post in what is now the parent's territory.

THE HALCYON BIRD

Kingfishers hunt by sight and therefore need clear water. They cannot cope with the turgid waters of the swollen river but must rely on the clearer shallow waters of the margins. When the river floods and spills over its banks fishing is difficult, and this is one of the times when kingfishers are better off resorting to nearby ponds and small watercourses. Despite all its talents even the halcyon cannot calm the troubled water! For the ancient Greeks, Halcyon the kingfisher had power over the wind and the waves; seven days before and after the winter solstice the birds nested, laying their eggs on the waves of the sea on a cradle of fish bones. Throughout this time the bird's powers produced a period of total calm and safety – the Halcyon days.

So in the halcyon river days of summer the jewelled kingfishers, most dazzling of all our birds, brighten and enliven the river banks, fishing the shallows, whistling their shrill claims to ownership and endlessly patrolling their river beat against intruders.

RIVERSIDE
OX-BOWS

The gradient is very shallow on the lowland river and its natural progression is by sinuous meanders across the plains. Nowadays some of the meanderings are almost inevitably under a degree of man-made control, but it is never possible to contain the river completely. The forces of the river oblige it to move in a certain way. As it has wandered back and forth across the valley it has left behind a legacy of old ox-bow lakes. Some have been filled in and absorbed into new fields but here and there they are marked by reedy, crescent-shaped pools or by the curved lines of old willows, poplars and oaks standing above the dark, uninviting waters. Some of the pools retain tenuous links with the river and become backwaters to it whenever the water levels rise; others only renew their link at times of flood and otherwise gain their own water supply by drainage from the surrounding fields or by virtue of the high water-table on the valley floor.

Whatever the reason, shape or form of these ox-bows they are diverse and important areas of quiet water lying close by the river. They quickly develop a thick fringe of vegetation and become rich, sheltered oases for waterside birds. Reed buntings favour such places because there is abundant cover for nesting and a prolific crop of seeds and fruit from the rank plant growth. All buntings are primarily seed-eaters and although the reed bunting specializes in the fruits and seeds of marsh plants it is yet another bird which has demonstrated a modern ability to adapt from one type of habitat to another. In former times there was always a clear distinction between the rough, bushy areas along the margins of water which were the province of the reed buntings and the drier farmland sites favoured by the related yellowhammer. In the past four decades, during which the familiar yellowhammer has declined, the reed bunting has happily expanded into drier sites – probably induced to do so by the general reduction of its wetlands – and has thereby succeeded in maintaining its numbers by increasing its range of habitats. Nowadays it is not restricted to the river bank and to reedy cut-offs, though its greatest numbers are still here.

REED BUNTINGS IN
SPRING

The female reed bunting is unprepossessing, one of the original small brown birds, best identified from other buntings by the fairly pronounced pattern of head markings. The cock bird certainly cannot be confused with any other and has a bold black head and throat, sharply defined white collar and moustacial stripe. Even in winter the patterning is distinct, although it is not as bright or conspicuous as it becomes in March or April when the pale tips of the feathers abrade to reveal the bold pied pattern on the head.

The reed bunting's song is one of the most tedious and monotonous sounds of the river bank, perfectly designed to drive the patient bankside angler or picnicker to distraction in the early months of summer. It is produced unceasingly, or so it seems, from mid-March onwards, and comprises two or three single notes with a slight pause after each (at every pause you pray it has lost its voice), followed by a jangling crescendo of unmusical notes. The male is evidently very proud of its rendering for its sits on the topmost spray of vegetation or on a bending reed, throwing its head high and shouting its song to the world. Eight or ten times each minute it may repeat the song, droning on for minute after minute and hour after hour.

Kingfishers pair for the
breeding season and
tunnel their nesting
chamber out of the soft
earth banks.

In one of the lines of oaks on a steep crescent of bank above an ox-bow, a dozen pairs of herons have their nests. Throughout the length of the river, from source to mouth, there are herons, but their heartland is here in the lowlands. This is where the hunting is best and most productive, the choice of site widest and the variety of food greatest. Though a fisherman, the best and

most practised on the river, even the heron does not live on fish alone. In fact its range of food is wide and often includes small mammals, birds, insects, crustaceans, reptiles and amphibians as well as fish. The shallow edges of the slow-moving river, and the pools, ditches, ox-bows and backwaters of the lowlands, are the ideal ground for the lank grey heron. Above all there are eels here and these are one of the greatest delicacies in a heron's diet.

Grey heron – never far away from the lowland river.

The heronry situated here is safe from human interference and is well placed to give the adult herons easy access to a wide choice of tested and traditional feeding sites. These are sites which are the exclusive property of the experienced adult birds of the colony; the most important individuals must have first call on the best feeding. Young and inexperienced birds have to make their own way in the hard world until, if they succeed and survive, their time comes to join a colony from which they can take advantage of these favoured sites.

So the lowland heron, grey, leisurely, but alert and highly efficient, patrols the river and its backwaters, pools and fields feeding on the prolific animal life produced by its waters and breeding in the high safety of the trees in its valley.

With long legs and long, spreading toes the herons are well equipped to move with ease amongst the vegetation of the river margin or on the flattened, decaying stems of floating marsh plants. They seem far less suited to arboreal nesting. They stand high in the crowns of tall trees incongruously gangling and unsteady, although, in fact, like many others of their kind which also nest in trees, they are perfectly at home; they grip the thin branches with long, strong feet and keep balance with ease even when the wild winds of March buffet the trees and the birds hunch up miserably, looking even more uncertain.

Herons nest early, well before the leaves are on the trees, and the flat stick nests are clearly visible. Once the young birds hatch, one of the adults remains in attendance for the first month to brood the chicks and shelter them from heat and rain. The young herons are insatiable and call for food incessantly. They will grasp the parents' bills hard and tug at them to stimulate the regurgitation of food. By the end of a month the bill-grasping and tugging by the growing offspring is so ferocious, the young birds pulling the adults' heads down to the floor of the nest, that no parent bird in its right mind – however devoted – will spend more time than necessary at the nest. Thereafter the adults visit only to deliver food.

By mid-June the young herons are leaving the nest and before summer has fully arrived the heronry is silent again and deserted until the following February.

These quiet backwaters of the ox-bows are one of the breeding areas for another large waterbird, the Canada goose. These geese, native to North

CANADA GEESE, COLONIAL RESIDENTS

America where they are highly migratory birds, were introduced into Britain as ornamental waterfowl on large private estates as long ago as the seventeenth century. Gradually they have become established in the wild; they have subsequently colonized much of lowland England and still continue to spread. They are particularly numerous in Norfolk, Yorkshire and the West Midlands. Although they are introduced aliens and cause some local concern where they graze densely on the best pastures in spring and summer, they are cautiously welcomed and do at least provide the birdwatcher with an opportunity to see 'wild' geese in the inland countryside.

They build their nests on the ground, usually close to the water in the lee of a low bush, fallen log or flood wrack. The gander in particular is an aggressive bird and its main defence against either two-footed or four-footed intruders approaching the nest or otherwise threatening is to attack. The attack can be of serious intent and genuinely daunting. I have watched a man prostrated by the fury of a low-level flying attack of a gander near the nest-site on river shingle. As the gander passed over and the intruder stood up the gander banked, swung round, levelled off to zero altitude again and repeated the attack from the other quarter to exactly the same effect!

The British population of this large, handsome goose is strongly sedentary, except for an interesting moult migration of non-breeding birds which has developed within some parts of the population. It is a northward migration undertaken in June solely for the purpose of moulting; strangely enough, it is precisely paralleled by the ancestral moult migration which the native population of North America makes each June. This movement of British birds has developed only in the past three decades and did not occur during the first two hundred years or more after the birds were introduced. Non-breeding birds from Yorkshire, and more recently from other areas as well, migrate to

Introduced Canada geese now breed widely in lowland England and Wales.

the Beauly Firth north of Inverness and remain there from June to August, by which time the moult is complete and the birds return south. The breeding birds, by definition, cannot join this moult migration because they are committed to rearing their young, so they moult on their breeding areas. During this time they are completely flightless for three to four weeks, regaining their powers of flight at the same time as the young birds reach the flying stage.

RETURN OF THE NORTHERN WADERS

As water levels lower in the ox-bows at the height of summer the exposed mud on the margins attracts the first of the northern waders returning from their Arctic and sub-Arctic breeding areas. There are several species which either shun saltwater – wood sandpiper, ruff, green sandpiper, spotted redshank – or are equally happy with either saltwater or freshwater and often appear inland on passage at this time of year: greenshank, black-tailed godwit, dunlin. The first birds to arrive, in the second half of July, may well be individuals which were unsuccessful in finding a partner or failed in their breeding attempt and therefore had no reason to remain on the breeding grounds. Some of these early arrivals will still be in their breeding dress, which is developed once they are on their breeding grounds and which we do not otherwise usually have the opportunity of seeing on either spring or autumn passage.

The spotted redshank is perhaps the most striking of these summer waders, dusky black plumage spangled with white on the upper parts and with vermilion legs and bill. The wood sandpiper, too, is spangled with white on the upper parts but against a very different olive-brown background. It is a delicate and slim bird, not as robust as the slightly larger and darker green sandpiper. The latter is the most common amongst this array of waders that appear at the ox-bow sites; although they occur singly, or at most in small parties of two or three, overall they are numerous in late summer in lowland river valleys throughout the country, appearing at innumerable individual sites, including the smallest farm ponds.

PALE AND GRACEFUL GREENSHANKS

The greenshank – tall, graceful and pale, with long, slightly upturned bill and green legs – is another passing migrant which is common on the riverside and on ox-bows in July and August. It is a distinctive bird with pale grey upper parts (even paler in winter), white underparts and a clear ringing call: '*tew, tew, tew.*' Greenshank nest on the wild, boggy moorlands and flows of northern Scotland – probably 700–800 pairs – but most of the passage birds in summer and autumn are from Scandinavia, where as many as 100,000 pairs breed.

Of all the riverside birds, the one which is most likely to be heard and not seen is the shy, elusive and murderous water rail. This small, lithe and creeping marshland bird is equipped with long, slender legs and toes that enable it to walk with ease on a floating mat of decaying vegetation, and it has

Spotted redshank (upper bird) and wood sandpiper are two of the earliest returning passage waders in late summer.

Quiet water edges in the ox-bows attract greenshank in July and August.

78

WATER RAILS,
ARCHETYPAL
MARSH BIRDS

a narrow, sinuous body for weaving in and out among the vertical stems of reeds and other marsh plants. Seldom seen and little known, the water rail lives mostly in the depths of wetland cover. Despite a weak appearance and a feeble flight it is quick and agile, with a long, darting bill; it feeds on a catholic range of water insects – caddis, dragonflies, waterbugs, beetles and craneflies, among many others. Although it eats a certain amount of plant shoots and roots it is principally carnivorous and any animal of sufficiently small size is fair game to a water rail. Water shrews, voles, frogs, small fish, marsh nestlings, eggs and crayfish are all eaten; animals are first killed by repeated blows to the back of the skull before being swallowed whole.

Outside the nesting season water rails are solitary and anti-social birds, openly aggressive to their own kind and pretty intolerant of other marsh birds as well. They will try to establish exclusive winter territories within which there are several favoured feeding areas linked by well-marked paths which they use to a fairly steady daily pattern. Once again it becomes apparent that there is nothing haphazard about the strategy which birds employ for making sure that ends meet throughout the difficult winter months of the year.

Water rails are also noisy, which is the most frequent reason for their presence being revealed to birdwatchers. They have a wide vocabulary of discordant grunts and squeaks, but the most frequent note, known as 'sharming', is a low, gutteral grunt which terminates as a hideous, pig-like squeal. Variously described as 'heart-rending', 'spine-chilling', 'disturbing' and 'diabolical', it takes a steady heart to hear the agonizing scream from the silence of a marsh at dusk and not miss a beat.

Where water meadows and old pastures remain beside the river colourful yellow wagtails may sometimes be found in summer. From mid-April onwards successive waves of these trans-Saharan visitors arrive on the south

Water rails are skulking marsh birds which seldom appear in the open.

coast of England and fan out into the wet lowland pastures of England and the Welsh borders. They are not universally distributed throughout the lowlands, however, and are absent from many areas which might appear to us to suit their needs.

Yellow wagtails are delicate, beautiful birds and the brilliant colour of the males is at its very best at the time of their arrival, an almost unbelievably dazzling canary yellow. They have a light and buoyant flight like other wagtails. As they flit from place to place they fan the black tail and display the white marginal feathers while they balance on the swaying heads of thistles or docks. They are indeed one of the golden gifts of summer in the riverside meadows.

CATTLE MEADOWS AND YELLOW WAGTAILS

They particularly favour cattle-grazed meadows and freshwater grazing marshes, where docks, thistles and ragwort typify the taller plants ignored by cattle and sheep. The wagtails build their nests in shallow depressions in the ground, often in the shelter of one of these plants, and through the breeding season the male spends much time on guard, sitting atop one of the tall stems or on a nearby fence post or wire. The song is undistinguished – but then who needs song when the plumage is as spectacular as this? The species is much more readily recognized by the familiar '*sweep*' anxiety-and-contact call which it uses at the slightest excuse.

Like all wagtails, this is a quick and nimble bird, feeding on winged insects in the short grass or pursuing them in brief, dainty excursions on the wing. It walks with a brisk gait and delights to feed amongst grazing stock, where it profits from the insects which the animals disturb as they move through the pasture. At the end of the breeding season the wagtails gather in sizeable flocks and then move away surprisingly quickly; by the end of August the river pastures are deserted and many of the birds have already left the south coast of Britain for Africa.

On the quieter stretches where the lowland river is wide and where the emergent growth of reeds, clustered club-rush, bulrush or bur-reed provides cover for nesting the handsome great crested grebes may be found. Although they are most typical of large sheets of open water – gravel-pits, lakes and reservoirs – they have increased in recent years and regularly make use of peaceful reaches. The excavation of many gravel-pits in lowland England since the Second World War has provided new habitats which the grebes have been quick to exploit. However, their recent success is a vastly different story to that which applied a century ago.

THE FORTUNES OF THE GREBES

The great crested grebe is almost too handsome for its own good and in the middle of the nineteenth century there was a vogue for 'grebe furs' in the fashion trade. To satisfy this quirk of fashion not only were grebe feathers imported from the Continent but in 1857 there began a massacre of British grebes so comprehensive that only three years later fewer than fifty pairs were left in the country, mainly on private waters where shooting was prohibited. Protection Acts from 1870 to 1880 improved the situation and finally gave them full protection in the breeding season. From its nadir around 1860 this elegant bird has recovered its ground and prospered far beyond all possible expectation, and current figures reveal that there are now approximately five thousand grebes in Britain.

The grebe is not a skulking bird, but spends its time conspicuously out on the open water. It is wholly adapted to aquatic life. Its legs are set so far back on its body that whereas they are ideal for propulsion they are hopelessly inefficient for walking, with the result that the bird rarely comes on land – nor, indeed, has it any need to do so. The nest, built up as a semi-submerged mound of vegetation, is secured amongst the new growth of stems of aquatic plants. Sometimes it is well concealed but at others it is well out in the open on the edge of the reeds, clearly visible.

Great crested grebes occur on slow, quiet sections of the river.

For many river birds with tiny young on the water the main threats of predation may well come not from above but from under water. Pike are the first enemy of the grebe broods, as they are for moorhen, coot and many species of duck. The adult grebes are proof against attack and they have evolved a special strategy to help ensure the safety of their young. Often in the early weeks after hatching the chicks will ride on the backs of the parents, thereby securing them from underwater attack, but also the two adults divide the brood between them, each taking full responsibility for one, two or three youngsters, as the case may be. Once this splitting of the family has taken place the bond develops between each adult and its respective siblings rather than between male and female as it was earlier in the breeding cycle; an adult will now have no further contact with the other young, nor with its mate, and will readily display open hostility and aggression if they approach. Even within its own sibling responsibilities the adult shows partiality, strongly favouring one of the offspring, usually the larger and better developed one, to the detriment of the rest. Harsh though it may seem, in this way the chances of at least one young bird attaining adulthood are maximized; the less fortunate young become the expendible reserve, the 'twelfth man' in the struggle for the success of the species over and above the interests of the individual. In seasons of plenty both may survive.

DIVISION INTO ONE-PARENT FAMILIES

An adult grebe needs somewhere in the order of half a pound (8 oz) of food each day. Great crested grebes are alone among British grebes in being principally fish-eaters, and they hunt by submerging from the surface and pursuing prey with powerful thrusts of their lobed feet. Each dive, be it exploratory or in pursuit, lasts less than half a minute and although they can apparently operate down to depths of eighty feet in extreme circumstances the birds normally fish in water 6–12 feet deep. They specialize in the slower-

moving fish such as roach, gudgeon, perch, tench, bleak and rudd, but also eat numbers of sticklebacks and minnows. Smaller fish are swallowed underwater but large ones are brought to the surface, held just behind the head and then manipulated in the bill so that they can be devoured head-first and alive.

Sand martins and swallows hunt insects over the river and its meadows.

CHIFF-CHAFFS, HERALDS OF SPRING

One swallow doesn't make a summer, but in much the same way as the song of the arriving chiff-chaff is the vocal herald of spring, so is the sight of the first sand martins scudding up and down the river, visual confirmation that the last throes of winter are passing. The sand martins are birds of the lowland river *par excellence*. Their association with rivers is more to do with nesting than with food supply (it happens to be convenient for them to collect food over water although it can almost as easily be found elsewhere, and often is). Their specialized need is for soft earth banks in which to excavate their nesting burrows and such sites can readily be found in the low, vertical banks on stretches of the slow-moving river. They will return each year to the same area of river to breed (young birds, too, return to the vicinity of their natal area) but they have to be opportunistic because the nature of their nest-sites – not only in river banks but also in sand pits, and so on – means that many will have crumbled by the next season and must be started again.

Each nesting tunnel is excavated by the pair themselves, hacking at the soft, sandy soil with bills that appear to be pathetically weak and inadequate for the task. Loose soil is pushed backwards and ejected from the burrow with the use of feet and it takes the pair several days to complete a horizontal tunnel 2–3 feet long. The chamber at the end is lined with grasses and feathers collected in flight and 4–5 white eggs are incubated for about fourteen days. They are normally double-brooded, therefore the breeding season extends well into July and August. Certainly along the lowland river there are

Although their bills appear weak, the sand martins have no difficulty digging burrows in the sandy river banks.

THE RISE AND FALL
OF THE SAND
MARTINS

few prettier sights than the animated comings and goings, and the conversational chatter, of a colony of riverside sand martins.

The martins feed aerially on a wide selection of flying insects from families such as aphids, little lonchopterid and acalypterate flies and small beetles, amongst many others. These are mainly groups of insects which are in great abundance over farmland and pasture, playing fields and river bank, rather than those which are associated specifically with water. As birds which depend on a reliable source of flying insects, sand martins arrive perilously early in Britain to face the chill of spring and it is possible that the long series of cold, wet springs Britain has endured in recent years has contributed to the marked decline in the numbers of sand martins which has taken place. On the Welsh section of the Severn in 1969 there were 1,230 pairs nesting but by 1978 this had slumped to 440 pairs. Similar levels of decline have been found in other parts of Britain and whereas the wet springs may have had a part to play the main reason is almost certainly related to the disastrous drought which has occurred every year from 1968 onwards in the wintering areas south of the Sahara. A modest recovery has taken place in the last few years and happily the sand martin is still a common bird on many of Britain's lowland rivers.

THE URBAN RIVER

Nowhere along its course is the river more confined and adapted than in its urban sections. The extent to which each urban river is adapted varies a great deal: the number of permutations is equivalent to the number of riverside towns and cities themselves. But wherever they are, except in the most extreme examples of canalized or polluted rivers, birds will be there making use of the river.

The first fact that the urban birdwatcher recognizes is that provided food is available and breeding sites can be found the mere proximity of man is not in itself an inhibition to birds. There are endless examples of birds of many species living side by side with human beings far more readily and successfully than one would imagine after observing the same species in its more traditional rural setting. In the countryside a bird may well be timid or skulking, whereas in an urban setting the same bird may be totally confiding and trusting – mallard, moorhen and woodpigeon are three prime examples.

CO-EXISTENCE OF BIRDS AND MAN

The sweet Severn slides gracefully past the old cathedral cities of Shrewsbury, Gloucester and Worcester. These urban stretches are bird-rich and peaceful: the Severn is fortunate throughout its long course to the sea in avoiding the industrialization and accompanying spoilation which has afflicted most other large rivers somewhere on their course. Except for the fact that the Severn watered the very cradle of the industrial revolution on its banks at Ironbridge in Shropshire, it has escaped the ravages of less fortunate rivers. Throughout its course it retains much of the character one would best expect of a well-cared-for river.

Upstream where the river passes through the small towns along its banks the river birds take little notice of the urban nature of their surroundings.

URBAN RIVER BIRDS

Here dippers pass, calling, up the river and mute swan, mallard, moorhen and even cormorant feed on the quiet sections; grey wagtails and kingfishers breed and feed here, and otters regularly pass through the town, pausing to leave their signal spraints on boulders beneath the spans of the town bridge.

In winter the rocky channel is swept clean by the racing river, cleared of all the debris and the remains of the lush vegetation of summer, its banks tidy and manicured and its waters flowing unimpeded on their course. In summer it has a very different image. Tall, waving heads of reed grass grow in the extensive shallows, emerging from amongst the crevices of the bedrock as a chain of waving islands on the side of the crystal river. Bright golden clumps of marsh marigold and patches of yellow spearwort line the river, later to be replaced by tall strands of hemp-agrimony and vivid splashes of purple loosestrife.

By May and June the channel itself is transformed. In the shallow areas its surface becomes an emerald green mat of trailing, swaying tresses of water crowfoot, brilliant with the thousands of glorious small white flowers pattern-

If it is in the right place, one perch is as good as another for the urban kingfisher.

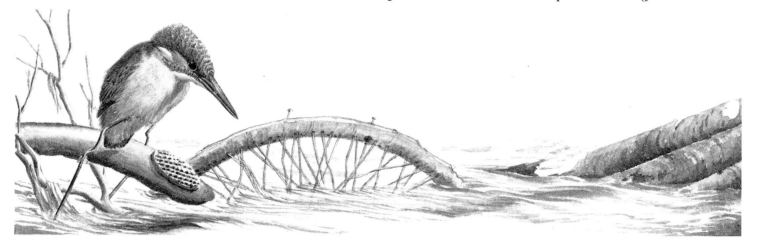

ing the mat. Each individual flower-cup floats delicately on the water and amongst this mass of colour the pied wagtails flit and skip on the surface, picking insects from the sparkling waters all through the long, summer days.

The summer river is a rich source of easy feeding for pied wagtails.

The waters flow shallow and warm and the daytime river is full of children and their games; later the fishermen take over, casting flies in the pools in the cool evening light. None of this welter of activity deters the urban wagtails, for this is their stretch of river too, shallow and alive with myriad insects. When the river is too busy they feed on the mown grassland of the town park, dancing into the air to catch flying insects and running in quick bursts to pick up others in the short grass. They have a nest right on the river bank, hidden amongst the rocks in one of the protective wire-mesh gabions below the walls of a warehouse in a short, quiet stretch of the river.

THE URBAN WAGTAIL

The pied wagtails are real companions of man, profiting far more from the association than any other wagtails do. Although they frequent watercourses they are not dependent on them in the way that the grey wagtail is. They fare well in farmyards, town parks, playing fields and gardens and are one of the species that has adapted particularly well to urban life. Like starlings, they have discovered not only the feeding opportunities that an urban environment can provide but also that in winter it is often advantageous to roost in towns and cities, where in hard weather the temperature will remain one or two critical degrees higher than in the surrounding countryside. Concentrations of roosting pied wagtails are commonly found in buildings and trees in numerous large conurbations; they also use the insides of factories, railway stations and even glasshouses!

In winter the hours of daylight are short and the organization and intensity of feeding for the wagtails has to be extremely efficient. It has recently been shown that pied wagtails have two principal alternative strategies for winter feeding. Either they remain in their flocks, concentrating their feeding in particularly rich and reliable sites such as sewage farms, flooded pastures and refuse tips, and moving from site to site if they need to; or they will set up their own exclusive waterside territories, just as they do when breeding in spring and summer. They will defend these against all others of their own species and also against any other insect-eating species which intrudes. The secret success of the individual's riverside territory at a time of year when insects are scarce relies on the fact that the river itself constantly delivers its own renewable supply of tiny insects.

Meadow pipits are not tolerated on the waterside by territorial pied wagtails.

A STRATEGY FOR WINTER FEEDING

On its individual stretch of river bank a wagtail walks the water's edge systematically, searching for items which the river has washed on to the tideline. Once the bird has covered one stretch the supply is depleted but by the time it has completed its circuit and returned to its starting point the river will have provided another supply just sufficient to furnish the needs of the bird. The size of a bird's territory is therefore critical. Any intruding bird feeding on waterside insects – pied wagtail, grey wagtail, dunnock or meadow pipit – will upset the delicate balance of supply and demand and must therefore be evicted as soon as it arrives. Skirmishing is often frequent but is expensive in energy consumption at a time of year when the balance between energy required and energy available is very fine. The wagtail must in any case feed continuously for about 90 per cent of the daylight hours simply to meet its normal daily energy needs.

If supplies within the territory become too sparse the owner will leave temporarily and join the flock. Conversely, if mild weather or any other factors produce a ready surplus on the river edge the territory-owner will, surprisingly, allow in a second bird to share the supply for a few days, evicting it again when necessity dictates. This improbable situation actually has benefit without detriment, for the owner receives help in defending the territory, which enables it to improve its own feeding rate and intake!

MALLARD, THE URBAN WATERFOWL

The pied wagtail is frequently an urban bird but far and away the most numerous river bird in most towns and cities is the mallard. Many of the individuals may originate from captive birds and those released on town lakes, but the familiar and popular mallard prospers well in built-up areas. The mallard is the most numerous, widely distributed and best-known of all European wildfowl. In Britain it is only in the depths of some industrial areas and on the bleakest of hill areas that it does not occur at all.

Mallard are very early nesters and once the ground temperature has risen above freezing they will begin to breed. Nests may be found from the end of February or early March, but the rural pairs have a high price to pay for these early-season attempts as ground cover is poor at the end of the winter and predation by foxes and crows is very heavy. Urban pairs, many of which do not

Mallard – the most numerous and familiar of urban wildfowl.

have to contend with the same number of predators, fare better in the early season. Mallard typically nest on the ground amongst a tangle of bracken, brambles or nettles where the female's dun colours give maximum camouflage. Females will select a variety of other types of site, however, and it is not infrequent for them to use tree sites, in the top of a pollard willow or in hollows on the inside of a shattered trunk. Here they are safer from predators and have a greater chance of success. However, on one recent occasion when a local farmer on his seasonal round of carrion crow nests discharged a shotgun into the base of nests high in the trees, a startled duck mallard rocketed pell-mell out of one of them. Later inspection showed the clutch of eggs to have been unharmed. This nest was 46 feet high!

Mallard ducklings leave the nest, wherever it is sited, on the day of hatching, so the vertical aerial descent of downy day-old ducklings from this nest would have been a sight to see!

Mallard form their pairs as early as September and once formed they remain together until mating takes place and the clutch is completed. Thereafter the male's task is done and he has no further function in the breeding cycle. In most bird species it is important that the pair remains together throughout the rearing of young but with mallard (and most other ducks) the pair-bond now breaks up and the male departs to the nearby river or town lake. There he will consort with other males, whiling away the spring and summer at a season when food is readily come by and living is easy. The number of males to be found at these times gives a good indication of the total of nests in the area.

In these built-up surroundings mallard are birds of the large waterways – not modest streams like the Rae in the middle of Birmingham, where a very different scene presents itself.

Blackbirds, chaffinches and house sparrows use the riverside alders even in the heart of industrial areas.

92

The river Rae rises and winds its way gently northwards to join the river Tame close to the arches of 'Spaghetti Junction', where the M6 curves east across the Midland plain towards the distant M1. This is no ordinary clear and rural brook. For ten miles of its twelve-mile course the Rae passes through the vast built-up area of Birmingham and its environs. This, the second largest conurbation in the land, has grown up on the banks of this small insignificant stream. Throughout almost all its course it is the epitome of an urban river, flanked by housing estates, factories, warehouses, motorways and canals, and it passes through the very heart of the city itself. It is about as unpromising a prospect for waterside wildlife as one could expect to find. However, even here the urban river defies all the odds and supports a flourishing wildlife community.

Within two miles of its source in the Lickey Hills the diminutive Rae has already crossed the only open countryside it will encounter and now passes through Longbridge and alongside the huge Leyland car works. In Longbridge, amid the 24-hour clamour, fever and intensity of a great industrial heartland, the Rae produces its first surprise for here, in Millwalk, is the only little ford remaining in the whole urban area of the west Midlands. Above the ford and the small footbridge alongside it the stream runs through manicured lawns in the grounds of the big Kalamazoo works, but there is a line of old alders left along the tidied channel of the stream which stood there long before the works was built. Chaffinches, blackbirds, house sparrows and even redpolls use the trees, dropping down to the water edge to drink. Downstream from the ford a rough grassy area twenty or thirty yards wide on either side flanks the stream for several hundred yards. It is scattered with hawthorn scrub, broom bushes, willow herb and beds of nettles, comprising an open corridor, delightfully unkempt and pristine, in the heart of the otherwise

UNEXPECTED
VISITORS

regimented city landscape. Dunnocks, blackbirds and wrens breed in the thickets, woodpeckers visit the dead trees and speckled wood butterflies dance in the grimy sunlit glades in summer.

Where the stream passes under the footbridge and fans out over the concrete ford to become temporarily 10–12 feet wide the water is shallow. The bed of the stream itself is stony and pied wagtails (together with one or two grey wagtails in winter) regularly spend their time here. They feed on the stony water edge gleaning insects brought down by the river. Astonishingly, too, dippers occur from time to time in winter, presumably wandering youngsters from the breeding streams in Shropshire and Worcester. Despite the urban nature of the little stream there are plenty of caddisflies, mayfly larvae and stoneflies, and a host of other aquatic invertebrates: turn over half-brick or a piece of tile on the bed of the stream (the insects do not differentiate between these and the natural stones in the rural brooks!) and they are there on almost every one.

A mile further on the Rae, still only 5–6 feet wide, meanders alongside the edge of playing fields for 400 yards. From its appearance it seems unlikely that it has ever been altered or adapted on this stretch; a line of old willows and elms – the latter mainly dead now – and stumpy alders trace the wandering course of the river. On the nearside it is light and open with a narrow, straight-edged margin of rough grass between the playing field and the stream, but on the far bank the ground is smothered with ivy which spreads upwards to cover the fence and several of the trees. It is dark under the canopy and the brooding shadow of a faceless factory, secure behind the high fence only twenty feet from the stream, blots out any other backdrop. The factory belches noise, hissing steam and grey smoke twenty-four hours a day. Exposed roots on the bank of the little stream, fallen branches and overhang-

Wrens are numerous amongst the thickets and tree roots on the river bank.

CITY KINGFISHERS

ing hawthorns have plucked sheets of plastic and polythene from the passing waters and now hold them suspended high above the surface.

Despite all these handicaps the Rae produces another jewel, for here under the trailing tresses of ivy on the far bank of one of the little meanders, deep in the earthy bank, kingfishers nest. A trickle of red soil running down the vertical bank and covering the slimy green carpet of mosses and liverworts betrays the presence of the nest hole. So, as well as a healthy insect population, the Rae has fish in it too, adequate at least to keep a pair of kingfishers and their young here deep in the heart of the city. There are plenty of dead branches littering the brook to provide perches for the birds but the king-fishers' favourite perch, just outside their nesting hole, is nothing more ele-gant than a semi-submerged red mudguard in mid-stream. Such urban refuse littering the stream may offend the human eye but for the kingfisher no aesthetic judgements are necessary: if it is in the right place, one solid perch is just as good as any other.

A bird arrives, hurtling round the bend of the stream low over the water and lands on the mudguard. It calls loudly with a double-note whistle to announce its arrival and proclaim the territory. Its mate slips out from the nesting hole, pauses for a moment on the red mudguard to shake itself, and flies away downstream. The kingfisher watches the female go and then flies upwards under the low bank and disappears inside.

Wychell Reservoir is derelict now, ten acres or so of willow carr, marsh and oily-black bulrush lagoons, lying behind its broken dam with the raised banks of the Rae forming its southern boundary. The railway line, an arterial road, housing estates and huge industrial works surround it on four sides, but of its type – a derelict wetland in the heart of the city – it is a gem. On a bright, clear day in February great tits and robins are already singing desultory songs

Robins and great tits – common birds in the riverside trees.

95

Little grebes, although shy birds, are at home on quieter urban waters.

in the bramble-swathed willow trees. A party of greenfinches work their way from tree to tree, blackbirds speed low from the safety of one cover to another and reed bunting, dunnock, blue-tit, wood pigeon and starling all contribute to the general air of activity. Sure enough, a snipe rises from the wet, marshy ground and twists away across the railway line. This is regular hunting territory for sparrowhawks, and water rail, too, must occur frequently in this ideal place.

COOTS AND THE BLACK LAGOON

The black, evil-looking lagoon is fringed with bulrush and reed and has an outer ring of willow carr secluding it from the rest of the marsh. The lagoon is a classic defiled urban pool, liberally scattered with old prams, chairs, supermarket trolleys, tyres, car doors, drums and other urban paraphernalia. It appears to be utterly sterile, polluted and unsavoury but in fact it is not because on its two acres twenty or thirty coot and a handful of moorhens subsist through the winter. Several of the coot pair together and stay to breed. Even here, against all the odds, in the darkest and most forbidding pool the waters produce enough life throughout the year to sustain these birds.

The reservoir was once a canal feeder, fed itself by the waters of the Rae on its southern side. These city canals, part of a huge network of waterways which were once the essential transport system of the Midlands and other new industrial areas, still remain although their primary purpose has gone. The long, straight channels and wide basins of the canals are favourite angling places and they also support modest numbers of water birds when undisturbed. Mallard, black-headed gulls, moorhens, occasionally tufted duck, and mute swans use them, and so too does the diminutive dabchick.

DABCHICKS, SMALLEST OF THE GREBES

This is the smallest of the grebe tribe; the shallow, muddy-bottomed canals suit its needs well, for it is a bird which lives on aquatic insect larvae, crustaceans and small fish which it prefers to seek in water no deeper than about three feet. It swims high in the water and dives with an arched jump and a splash; being particularly good at concealment, when disturbed it will quickly hide, for long periods if necessary, in the bankside vegetation.

One final indignity overtakes the Rae in the brick and concrete heart of its city. Below the little red inspection doors on the bridge in Fazeley Street in Digbeth the Rae swirls through a half-moon brick-built channel between walls twenty feet or more high, devoid of life and spirit. This is the urban river under man's command, if not under his total control, for even here from time to time it strikes back. There is no soil, nor any shoulder of land over which to spill, and in times of flood the channelled river becomes a sweeping devil rising as much as six feet in twenty minutes. In this way it has already claimed the lives of city children innocently playing in its bowels.

The only visible sign of the river having any connection with natural life in this section is the small pile of sticks and leaves which it has swept down with it and which lodge against the piers of the bridge where the culverted stream curves out of sight again. Yet even here there is bird activity: city sparrows and feral pigeons drop down into the channel from the high walls above to drink and bathe on the edge of the water. Moreover it is strongly asserted by the office workers whose windows look out from the high walls above the concrete channel that in summer the kingfisher flies the city stream. Here it passes, a flash of electric blue emerging from the dark river tunnel, speeding under the road bridge and rounding the bend to the more promising open ground 400 yards downstream.

THE ROYAL BIRD

The mute swan is easily the best-known and most popular of river birds in Britain. It is a bird of superlatives, the largest bird in Britain, the most regal (in fact, the royal bird), one of the most admired, and probably the most physically daunting to its human neighbours. Its legendary size and dazzling white plumage make it unmistakable. It is a bird which prefers the slow-moving sections of lowland rivers as well as reservoirs, lakes, canals and estuaries, occurring even where there are tidal waters, and it is equally at home in urban and rural surroundings. Most of the mute swans in Britain are not truly native but originate from the semi-domesticated stock of the Middle Ages. Their original homeland was eastern Europe. The protection which was afforded them then, and subsequently the wider protection by royal decree, accounts for their great tameness and their lack of evident fear of humans.

These swans build large mounds of nests using the stems and leaves of water plants, and whereas they are too large and too conspicuous to attempt camouflage, they try to select sites which are inaccessible to vandals and foxes. Therefore they often build on river islands, in reed beds or by the piers of bridges, but this means there is quite a heavy loss of nests through flooding.

A female swan (pen) incubates and then broods the hatching young before they leave the nest.

Although mild and inoffensive most of the time, the cob will defend the nest-site with impressive determination and vigour whilst the pen carries out all the incubation by itself the cob guards the territory. The male's aggressive display is indeed impressive, with the wings arched over the back, neck feathers fluffed and head arched far back between the wings. In this position the cob thrusts across the water towards the intruder in strong pulsing jerks and is a pretty frightening sight. Many are the bathers, fishermen, boaters and picknickers each year who discreetly move on rather than face the intimidating threat display. Threat rarely develops into physical attack, certainly not against humans, but it is none the less prudent to regard an aggressive male swan with great respect and to remember the degree of physical damage that can be caused. The male swan's prowess as an adversary is demonstrated by the following incident.

In 1982 the female swan of a pair on a river in West Wales was killed by vandals. The male remained alone and by the onset of the next breeding season was clearly very frustrated and lonely. The only other large white objects anywhere in the area were the Welsh ewes and their lambs and it was to one of the ewes that the swan turned his attention, driving it into the shallows and attempting to mate with it. The ewe's twin lambs followed faithfully behind her, only to be regarded as competitors, and were killed outright by the swan, which simply picked them up in its bill and shook them to death. The ewe, unable to oblige the swan, met a similar end: not only was she found in the water, presumed drowned, but her neck was broken too. The facts of this remarkable incident are beyond dispute and the incident is as interesting for its rarity and improbability as for its illustration of the mute swan's enormous strength and power.

The moral of this story is that swans should be left well alone during the breeding season. Unfortunately in many urban areas they are badly persecuted and every year produces stories of appalling vandalism to breeding swans, usually by youths. The gracious swan, having been assiduously protected over the centuries, is now under constant threat from such delinquents in certain parts of Britain.

Mute swans' natural food is mainly submerged aquatic plants which they reach by up-ending in the water, but they also graze in wet fields and many are fed in towns and cities on regular supplies of bread. Yet, though popular and numerous, mute swans are currently facing severe problems and some serious local declines. Like many other birds, swans need to take supplies of grit into their gizzard to enable them to grind down the vegetable matter they have eaten before digestion. The current side-effects of this process are disastrous for swans.

Swans are part of the urban river scene in many towns and cities — London, Oxford, Chester, Nottingham — but few towns have a greater sentimental attachment to the birds than Stratford-upon-Avon, where they are a popular tourist attraction and greatly prized by local people. It was because of a serious decline in the number of swans at Stratford that a government enquiry took place in 1979 and the fuller picture of the demise of urban river swans became clear.

The Stratford flock of fifty to sixty birds each winter declined from 1965 onwards, until by 1978 there were only one or two left. On the Thames between 1823 and the 1950s the annual 'swan-upping' showed a population varying between 400 and 600 individuals. By 1969 it had risen as high as 1,200 only to crash to 153 by 1981. In 1956 about 200 pairs bred in the London area; by 1982 it had fallen to 44 pairs.

Investigation of dead swans has shown a variety of causes for premature deaths, including vandalism, overhead wires and entanglement with fishing line, but by far the most serious and insidious cause is progressive poisoning

Mute swans pair for life but strengthen their pair bond in early spring each year.

99

from lead picked up by swans in the form of lead shot spilled or discarded by anglers on the river bank or in the water margins. The lead shot is taken up in mistake for pieces of grit. It is now believed that about 3,000 swans per year die prematurely from this lead poisoning in the UK, out of a population of about 18,000 (1978). In 1982 and 1983 80 per cent of the 800 swan deaths examined in Norfolk and the East Midlands were caused by lead; on the Thames the figure was 60 per cent and in other parts of the UK 40 per cent.

In 1984, not a moment too soon, anglers are accepting alternatives to lead for use as weights, a code of conduct has been issued and posters warning of the grave dangers to birds of lead and discarded fishing line are being widely distributed.

THE HAZARD OF ANGLING REFUSE

It is not only swans that are vulnerable to the menace of discarded fishing line. Any bird which uses the riverside for any purpose is in potential danger. Members of the Young Ornithologists' Club collected over six miles of discarded nylon fishing line in nine months in 1978–9 (an average of over 800 feet of line per mile). Considerable numbers of birds are killed or maimed by this discarded line each year. Mallard and moorhen are amongst the most frequent casualties but a wide range of other waterbirds are affected – dippers, wagtails, grebes, herons – and other species varying from kestrel, meadow pipit and starling to tawny owl. The sight of a moorhen hopelessly entangled in fishing line, suspended from an inaccessible branch over the river Thames, is not one that is readily forgotten.

In other, completely different, ways a frustrated or impatient angler may occasionally look askance at the enviable skill and efficiency of some of his avian companions on the river, and may even ponder the degree of competition which he faces. Such skill should indeed be wondered at and admired because, unlike the human angler who fishes purely for recreation, the birds are obliged to be infallibly successful day after day if they are to survive. For this reason, throughout the ages evolution has honed and selected these skills to fit each species best for its own particular method of catching fish.

FISHING FOR FOOD OR SPORT

Although suspicion of unfair competition may understandably enter the angler's mind, the only genuine causes for worry occur very occasionally and almost without exception in circumstances where man himself has produced artificial conditions which are then exploited by birds.

For example, the commercial mass-production of fish in open pools or tanks at fish farms, or the stocking of lakes, reservoirs or rivers with well-grown fish on a 'put and take' basis, will almost always attract enterprising birds. In situations such as these any fish-eating predator worth its name will automatically attempt to take advantage of the sudden glut of potential food. In such situations the onus must lie with the managers to ensure adequate protection for such stocks or produce deterrents to keep bird predators at a

The kestrel is the most familiar bird of prey in town and countryside.

Even cormorants use the urban river where it is relatively undisturbed.

distance. However, birds have been – and still are in some areas – persecuted for taking advantage.

Cormorants and goosanders, both now fully protected by law (although general licences to kill them have been issued by the Department of Agriculture in Scotland), are still quite widely shot inland. To redress the balance, however, at least one enlightened water authority (Welsh Water) has made it clear that it will not involve itself in any way in any proposals for the legal control (i.e. licensed slaughter) of cormorants or other avian fish predators. Although goosanders are quite widely – and illegally – shot in northern England and parts of Wales, they have so far shown a commendable capability to withstand even fairly heavy persecution.

ILLEGAL KILLING OF FISH-EATING BIRDS

Human frustration, even if misplaced and unfair, can perhaps be understood, for whereas the game fisherman must use rod, line, fly and intuition, plus acquired experience, to attempt to catch trout or salmon, the goosander – lithe and electric-fast in pursuit – slips under the water and pursues small fish in the clear waters with perfect vision and a pressing mortal intent.

Even small birds such as kingfisher and dipper are said to have caused problems. Dippers have been accused of the destruction of fish eggs but there is no evidence to support this, and it is physically impossible for the bird to excavate the gravel of a salmon redd to reach the concealed eggs. It is quite conceivable that dippers consume eggs disturbed by other means, in which case the eggs would not hatch anyway and the dippers can hardly be blamed for taking advantage of the surplus.

Kingfishers subsist almost entirely on small fish of minnow size. They are highly territorial, each pair's territory being up to a mile in length – within which distance it is inconceivable that the birds can have any effect whatever on the total fish populations.

Riverside trout farms occasionally attract the attentions of passage ospreys en route to or from the northern breeding areas of Scotland. Such birds are capable of taking – and indeed prefer – large fish of about 2 lbs weight. Understandably, they can be a source of irritation to a trout-farm owner who sees a bird taking up residence for a few days, making repeated forays to the fish tank to collect easy prey. But the ospreys' visits are short-lived and some of the fish-farm owners admit not only to tolerating but actually to enjoying the occasional visit of an osprey!

HERONS AND FISH FARMS

The principal conflict between fishing birds and commercial fish-rearing, however, centres once more on the grey heron. The species is well-known to frequent garden ponds, and sometimes to empty them of goldfish or other stock, and it is irresistibly drawn to fish farms, with their tanks and pools pulsing with fish of different sizes. In an attempt to help produce recommendations on how to alleviate the problem without resorting to shooting (which is in any case illegal), the RSPB carried out a detailed examination of the problem in 1979–80. This revealed that predation at fish farms is widespread, and that most visits by herons take place in the very early morning and the late evening. Moreover, a high proportion of visiting herons in summer are young birds, newly fledged from heronries, or sometimes dispersing young from further afield which are wandering in search of good feeding and find such places by chance.

The RSPB study showed that the various systems of caging, scaring devices and wires that impede access to the shallow water at the edges of the pools could be effective. Pool design is also important, because herons always land on the bank edge and walk into the water – but if the pools are deep-sided and the water is therefore out of reach the herons will be reluctant or unable to fish.

Herons are breeding birds in a surprising number of towns and cities.

Occasionally passage osprey linger to exploit the easy fishing at trout farms.

Like most other birds the herons moult their flight feathers one by one at the end of the breeding season, gradually to replace them with new, strong ones: wildfowl – ducks, geese and swans – are exceptions to this normal pattern of moulting and pass through a period of total flightlessness.

ECLIPSE PLUMAGE Drake mallards become less evident in June each year. Having left the incubating of eggs and rearing of young entirely to the ducks the males' duties are finished; one of the results of this is that they go into a full moult a month or so earlier than the females. During this moult the birds lose all their flight feathers virtually simultaneously and are thus rendered flightless for several weeks. Throughout this period of moult the familiar bright colours are completely lost and the drake mallard – like other duck species – passes through a much duller eclipse plumage. The birds become skulking and withdrawn at this period and spend most of their time out of sight amongst the emergent plant growth of summer. They closely resemble the females for this short season and adopt the cryptic, or camouflage, colouring to make them less visible at a time when they are at their most vulnerable.

Males of other duck species suffer similarly and sit out the weeks in the height of summer flightless, dowdy and secretive. The male tufted duck spends the period of eclipse disconsolately on the open water; he appears much like his mate but is darker, retaining the shadow of his purple glossed head and never showing the little patch of white at the base of the bill which characterizes the females. The pochard loses his glorious chestnut head temporarily but retains more than a suggestion of grey on the back and is not so readily confused with the female.

Even the gaudy and decorated mandarin becomes a barely recognizable shadow of himself. Gone is the long crest, the purple and copper shading, the orange 'side-whiskers' and the decorative chestnut 'sails'. He metamorphoses

into a slightly brighter version of the duck but the retention of the pink bill is a give-away at all times.

Wildfowl abound in London, including, in winter, smew, tufted duck, shoveler and gadwall.

Few rivers are more thoroughly urban over a long distance than the Thames as it twists and winds its way for fifty-five miles or so from the western suburbs of London all the way to Gravesend at the head of the estuary. Throughout almost the whole of this length the river – tidal for two-thirds of the way – is of little importance for breeding birds because the banks are completely built up on either side as far downstream as Barking Creek, near the huge Ford works at Dagenham where coastal marshes, rough grazing and drainage channels at last provide open ground again alongside the river channel.

The river banks may not offer much opportunity for birds to breed but the river itself supports surprising numbers and variety in this, the biggest conurbation in Europe. However, to build up a true picture of riverside birds in the capital it is necessary to consider the wider context of the tributaries which flow into the Thames, especially the Lea and Colne on the north and the Darent on the south. In these valleys, and along the western part of the Thames itself, huge areas of open water have been created through the construction of reservoirs (now over 4,500 acres) and the excavation of sand and gravel-pits. The combination of these, together with the existence of many artificial ponds and lakes in London parks, produces a wealth of urban water birds. As living proof of the fact that, given adequate food supply and available habitat, wild birds can tolerate extreme levels of human activity and proximity, it is now believed that in winter the London area (within a 20-mile radius of St Paul's Cathedral) holds 5 per cent or more of the total national populations of five species of wildfowl: namely, shoveler, smew, tufted duck, gadwall and goosander.

Male (top) and female gadwall

Gadwall

Great crested grebe (winter)

spring display of mandarin drake

Great crested grebe (first autumn)

Great crested grebe (summer)

female mandarin

(winter)

Little grebe (dabchick) (summer)

Urban wildfowl.

Several of the riverside reservoirs have become famous for their birds. At Walthamstow the heronry on islands in the reservoir is now one of the largest in Britain, with over a hundred nests; large numbers of shoveler, tufted duck (over 1,000 sometimes), and mute swans occur there and several pairs of pochard breed. Barn Elms reservoirs, lying at bend of the river at Barnes, also have large numbers of duck, several species of which breed, including the scarce gadwall. Concentrations of feeding swifts and house martins are also attracted in summer, and in recent years other breeding birds have included reed warbler, reed bunting, coot, moorhen, dabchick, great crested grebe and mute swan. All these are birds which most of us picture in our mind's eye in the quiet of the English countryside, and yet here at Barn Elms they are all breeding on the very edge of Inner London, within 4 miles of the city of Westminster!

MANDARINS,
AN ORNATE
INTRODUCTION

The ornate mandarin duck, a native of northern China, was introduced into this country earlier this century, soon after which some birds escaped from captivity to breed in the wild. Their main centre is in the valleys of the northward-flowing tributaries of Mole, Bourne and Wey, but they are expanding their range and numbers slowly so that odd birds appear with increasing regularity in other areas of London along the Thames and its tributaries. The mandarin is a tree-hole nesting duck and may be limited in its spread by the lack of suitable nest-sites, but it may be helped in its expansion by the provision of artificial nest-sites on man-made waters. The male in particular is an attractive and highly-coloured duck.

Canada geese: urban colonists quite unafraid of man.

Dabchick, great crested grebe, sand martin, reed warbler, sedge warbler, mute swan and Canada goose are all riverside birds which nest numerously on waters adjacent to the urban Thames and its tributaries. The little ringed plover turned up to breed in the Thames valley in Middlesex soon after it first

arrived to colonize Britain, and now occurs widely along river valleys in the London area. When the Surrey docks closed down little ringed plovers had colonized the site within three years! Now over sixty pairs breed in the London area each year.

In London between twenty and thirty pairs of kingfishers breed each year: one pair excavated a burrow at Kew, only a few miles from Central London, some years ago but left prematurely without succeeding; herons not only have their large colony at Walthamstow but also breed in Regent's Park, from where they either slip into the zoo to filch the fish that are provided for captive birds or fly across the heart of London to fish the creeks and wastelands of the derelict Surrey Docks area.

WILDFOWL ON THE THAMES MARSHES

Once the brick and concrete riverside has given way to wastelands and marshes at Barking, Rainham and Dagenham the concentrations of both breeding and wintering birds increase. On Rainham marshes and the river adjacent to it duck numbers are high in the winter months: there may be as many as 1,000 teal, 450 mallard, 600 shelduck, 100 wigeon, 100 pintail and 500 pochard at their peaks. Short-eared owls, flocks of lapwing and yellow-hammer, occasional snow buntings and other unlikely birds use these urban river marshes in winter. In summer several pairs of shelduck breed here, as do reed warblers, sedge warblers, corn buntings and yellow wagtails. Here at the head of the estuary the long river enters its final stage, where its rich waters will support a great welter of wildlife.

THE ESTUARY

Previous pages: grey geese, shelduck, redshank and black-headed gull epitomise the richness of the estuary as a bird-watcher's mecca.

The estuary is flat and wide and lonely, a haunting, two-dimensional wilderness. The river's energy is finally spent and as it spills into the estuary it no longer answers to the imperative of gradient but to the twice-daily orders of the tides. Here its precious load of fine muds and sediments is laid down in continual replenishment of the estuary's infinite fertility. Here the river undergoes its last transformation.

It is early March and at night there is a hint of spring warmth for the first time. Even now, far out on the edge of the flat, grey-green marsh the air has a gentle softness to it, replacing the stiletto sharpness of the past five months. As the first pale ribbons of day stretch across the lightening sky from edge to edge, no horizon is apparent: all distant perspective is lost, and on these outer reaches of the marsh only the running edge of the advancing tide marks a perceptible boundary. Beyond it the flat silkiness of dawn disguises the broad miles of the estuary waters and the merged slate-grey of the sky above: from tideline to sky limit is a single vault of grey.

In the calm of the dawn is nothing but stillness and silence. The only movement is the rippling lip of the tide as it creeps to the soft edge of the saltmarsh. But now curlews start to call, unseen, from the banks of spartina marsh downstream; their calls swell in number, so there must be many of them coming in to roost and shrouded by the half-light. The only other sound is the gentle hiss of the tide as it reclaims the last few hundred yards of wet grey mud. The smell of mud, earthy and elemental, spiced with the tang of salt, is ever-present; boot-clinging and plastic, it is the one constant element of the river estuary – more constant than the waters of the river themselves which ebb and flow twice every day, covering and uncovering the mud. The air is warm, but ahead of the advancing water edge a cold carpet layer rolls ankle-high across the marsh, an unseen tide of air pushed ahead by the insistence of the returning waters.

In the growing light seven shelduck, spectral-white and ethereal, sail by 400 yards off-shore. Erect and magisterial, they seem, uncannily, to be sailing half way up the sky above the imagined horizon of the waters.

THE RISING OF THE TIDE

Suddenly there are birds everywhere. Deprived of their feeding areas on the open mud by the engulfing water and pushed inexorably inshore by the running tide for the past four hours, dunlin are now on the wing. They arrive from farther up the estuary, swirling fast in a tight, compact flock of 3,000 or more. Deceptively two-dimensional on first sight, the dense flock has a mass and a being of its own. Each bird flies in the most perfect unison with all others as the mass twists, swirls and gyrates; it towers upwards, unwinds, stretches and contracts again and plummets seawards as each perfect high-speed manoeuvre is performed in consummate synchrony. Other distant flocks appear in the emerging background; like waving columns of smoke they

JOURNEY'S END

Strings of dunlin move inshore as the tide advances.

114

appear for a moment and then vanish suddenly as they turn their darker backs to the eastern sky. The nearest flock swings to and fro low over the last grey bands of exposed mud. As the dense cloud switches back and forth in perfect unison it is mirrored in the silver shallows of the tide. Each time that the flock swings pendulum-like, lower and lower, birds from the bottom of the pack land until after a dozen passes the last ones touch ground. As they do so the whole flock erupts again in a thundering, pulsating throng and races farther down the estuary where it settles first time without ceremony.

Redshank and turnstone are pushed off the mud flats by the rising tide.

No bird in the flock can keep still; they move or preen, or feed, or stretch and 'gape' – an agitated multitude of birds incapable of stillness. There are a few bigger birds amongst them, birds which flew on the periphery of the flock as they sped down the estuary. These are grey plover, hunched and dejected-looking, standing singly amongst the flock like bored chaperones for the effervescent mass of dunlin.

Farther along the marsh edge a close line of wooden posts runs low into the flooding tide, flat-topped and functionless. They are charcoal-black against the grey water and the outer ones have already quietly slipped below the silky, still surface of the tide. There are forty or more of these posts and on every one a bird is perched – redshank, grey plover and turnstone. The grey plover again stand still, hunched and silent; between them the redshank are flighty and agitated and their piping calls ring across the water. Mirror images reflect each bird and the outer ones, belly-deep in the rising flood, are forced to leave and then vie with their companions for the disappearing perches. A turnstone ousts a companion which overbalances into the deep water and, unexpectedly, swims with calm deliberation to the next post and springs nimbly, straight from the water, to contest another perch. Shortly they all give up. Rising in unison, they disappear up the estuary in a straggling line low over the water to await the ebb.

The enclosed estuary fields provide winter feeding for flocks of lapwing and golden plover.

ESTUARY GRAZING MARSHES

In the upper reaches of the estuary great flat salt-marshes extend either side of the river channel. Nearest to the channel the lower saltings are the grey-green of common saltmarsh grass, and in summer are suffused with a pink haze of sea spurrey and milkwort. Most parts of the upper saltings are heavily grazed by sheep or cattle, for the fescue grasses and bents are valuable and nutritious grazing. Around all the major estuaries of Britain – Wash, Thames, Severn, Solway and Forth – and many of the smaller ones, great droves of wildfowl share the winter grazing on these flat and fertile marshes. Even on the inland areas farthest from the river, where the marshes have long since been fenced off and hedged into broad wet fields, geese, ducks and packs of lapwing, golden plover and curlew congregate and feed, often in their thousands.

WILD GEESE

Once they have left their breeding grounds in Iceland, Arctic Europe, Russia, Greenland or Svalbard (Spitzbergen), the wild geese of the north move to the milder regions of western Europe for the winter. Some head inland, feeding on stubble, the residues of root crops or freshwater grazing meadows, but many make for traditional wintering grounds on the estuaries and estuary saltings. There is no more evocative sound in the bird world than the call of wild geese as they fly to and from the feeding grounds each day. At dusk and dawn they move from the safety of a night-time roost on the open water to feed through the hours of daylight. In long lines and in V-shapes the skeins cross the sky and drop down, wiffling and twisting to the chosen feeding areas. As they fly overhead their haunting calls distinguish them: the deep triple notes of greylags, '*gnong-ong-ong*' (identical to the call of the familiar farmyard goose which originates from them), the similar but less deep two-note call of pinkfeet, '*ank-ank*', and the higher-pitched '*kow-yow*' of whitefronts. The black and white barnacle geese are more vociferous than most of the grey geese, both on the ground and in flight, often keeping up a shrill yapping like a pack of small dogs; brent geese are more silent but sometimes clamorous in flight, making a confused, monosyllabic babble of sound.

The geese are wild and very wary; they use the visibility of the flat, open marsh as their safety or, if they feed in the enclosed fields of the estuary, it is only the largest and most open that they frequent. Birdwatchers normally see geese only from a distance; 800 yards through a telescope is close for a view of wild geese.

All round the British coast favoured estuaries provide winter feeding for these separate flocks. The outer reaches of the Thames estuary and its satellites support some 40 per cent of the world population of brent geese from breeding areas in Russia (a separate race breeds in Greenland and winters in Ireland). Other estuaries on the Essex coast – Blackwater, Colne, Hamford

Various types of geese, from the Arctic and from northern Europe, winter on British estuaries.

Greylag goose

Pink-footed goose

White-fronted goose (Siberian race)

Barnacle goose

White-fronted goose

Lesser white-fronted goose

Lesser white-fronted goose

White-fronted goose (Greenland race)

Lesser white-fronted goose

Water – and in north Kent also have flocks of 1,000 or more in mid-winter; this is a goose which has increased its numbers dramatically in recent years. Small, neat and black with a white 'necklace', they are geese which traditionally feed on mud flats below high tide where they graze the beds of thread-like eel grass (zostera). In recent years, as their numbers have doubled, they have extended their feeding to arable crops further inland. Between one and two thousand white-fronted geese also winter in the Thames estuary, usually on the north Kent marshes, and another of their regular areas in southern England is in the lower valley of the Hampshire Avon, which attracts several hundred birds.

Occasional rarities – such as the red-breasted goose – arrive with the flocks of whitefronts from the Siberian Arctic.

The Ribble estuary in Lancashire is another great goose area. It traditionally supports well over 10,000 pink-footed geese each year, although in recent years more and more of the birds have made use of inland roosts and arable fields. Over 75,000 pinkfeet winter in Britain, including the whole of the Iceland/Greenland population, but most of them are distributed over inland areas in the lowlands of Scotland where many of the greylag geese, too, are concentrated.

MARSHLAND GEESE

The vast marshes of the Solway on either side of the rivers Eden and Esk also attract huge numbers of pinkfeet, particularly when they congregate in later winter before returning north. Barnacle geese use these Solway marshes too, for the entire breeding population from the Arctic island of Svalbard comes to this one site – 6,000–7,000 birds each winter. There are excellent facilities for seeing these geese at the Wildfowl Trust's grounds at Caerlaverock on the Scottish side of the Solway.

These concentrations of geese are compulsive viewing for birdwatchers and nowhere do so many people see the flock of wild geese each winter as at the Wildfowl Trust at Slimbridge, on the upper reaches of the estuary of the river Severn itself. White-fronted geese from northern Russia come to the marshes and wet fields here between November and March and many thousands of people watch them from the wide range of ground-level and tower hides provided by the Wildfowl Trust. Sometimes here, as at other sites, unusual geese in the process of migration travel with the main flock and arrive here as stragglers, providing particular excitement for birdwatchers. Red-breasted geese and lesser whitefronts are the most likely varieties to become accidentally associated with the European whitefronts; both species normally winter in south-east Europe or the Caspian Sea area and are a thousand miles or more off-course when they turn up in Britain.

OTHER WILDFOWL OF THE GRAZING MARSHES

On all these estuary marshes and fields other wildfowl graze too. The musical whistling of male wigeon is one of the typical sounds. Like the geese, wigeon are communal feeders, often occurring in very large flocks. They graze the cropped sea-turf in tight groups or stretched out in long, straggling lines. In one wide field dotted with wet hollows and depressions they graze busily; each grazing group is strangely flat-topped as the birds reach forward and pull at the short turf, inching slowly forward in unison as they do so, with a rolling gait. Others stop to bathe and preen in the flashes and hollows of water. Lapwing, too, are using these fields, scattered loosely right across the open ground – not in a dense group as the wigeon are. In this field alone there are probably over 2,000 lapwing and among them a handful of golden plover too. Several hundred starlings probe the drier parts of the field, and curlew wander among the lapwings, probing the soft soil gently with long, curved bills. Their bill tips are surprisingly delicate and sensitive, ideal for feeling for the earthworms which they hunt. These are mainly male birds, whose bills are distinctly shorter than the females. Curlew prefer to feed on the open mud of the river's sides and the open estuary, where their long bills enable them to

The curlew's cry is the most evocative sound on the estuary.

117

probe deep for lugworms. These are considerably more nutritious than earth-worms but sometimes when hard weather or other circumstance puts them out of reach of the males' bills they are forced to go inland to feed on the more accessible but less nourishing earthworms, leaving the female curlew with their longer bills to continue exploiting the lugworms.

THE HIGH TIDE

When the tide is full and holds back the emptying waters of the river, many of the molluscs, crustaceans, annelid worms and other invertebrates which inhabit the mud in their millions emerge to feed. When they do so they are relatively safe from the wading birds which probe for them when the mud is exposed, but now other predators take over, those which can reach or dive through the muddy waters and hunt the floor of the estuary. Pintail, graceful ducks whose longer necks enable them to reach the bottom in deeper water than mallard or teal, feed on many hydrobia snails, shrimps and other small invertebrates as well as plant seeds. Many thousands of pintail winter in the estuaries of the rivers Mersey, Dee, Ribble, Medway, Stour and border Esk.

Red-breasted mergansers hunt the estuaries at high tide for flounders, gobies and coalfish. Eider, too, in the northern estuaries and inlets, dive to look for slow-moving or immobile creatures such as mussels, periwinkles, crabs and whelks. Scoter prefer sandier bays and estuaries and dive for cockles, mussels, clams and a variety of other shellfish. High tide is the time when cormorants pursue the founders, blennys, saithe and eels which re-appear in the estuary as the tide returns.

The fecundity of the estuaries is so vast that it is sometimes difficult to comprehend. The river brings with it a constant renewal of mud and sediments which make the estuary waters perpetually opaque and cloudy. In the Severn estuary alone it is calculated that there are least ten million tons of mud suspended in its waters at any one time. Incalculable amounts of plant

Eiders feed in the shallow waters of the rising tide.

and animal nutrients brought with this mud, together with mineral salts, make the estuary richly fertile. An acre of estuary mud is easily twice as productive as the very best agricultural land. The narrow range of plants and animals occurring in the estuaries is merely a reflection of the harsh environment in which they have to live – alternately wet and dry, subject to changes in salinity and open to extremes of weather and temperature.

Some pairs of ringed plover breed on the estuaries; many more use them as feeding sites when they are migrating.

THE LIVING MUD

The sheer numbers of some individuals living in the mud is staggering. The ragworm *Nereis*, 2–3 inches long, can occur at densities in excess of 2,500 per square yard; another segmented worm, *Pygospio elegans*, at 450,000 per square yard. *Hydrobia* snails are counted in thousands per square yard as are the tiny Baltic tellin, the shrimp-like *Corophium* and many others. Some of the creatures which are invisible to the naked eye, such as nematode worms, may exceed 10,000,000 per square yard! The estuaries are also immense spawning grounds, hatcheries and nurseries for other marine life, notably fish. In late summer and autumn many young fish re-enter the estuaries for the winter. On the upper parts of the Severn estuary a surprising total of almost 90 different species of fish have been recorded.

With such phenomenal productivity it is little wonder that the estuaries of British rivers (and others on the mild western seaboard of Europe) support such prodigious numbers of waders and wildfowl. At some seasons as many as two million waders at a time may be using the coasts of Britain. They roost in dense concentrations on salt-marsh or inland fields when the tide covers the estuary, but once it ebbs they move out once more on to the exposed mud to feed on the host of invertebrates it harbours.

The length of bill determines how each different bird species can feed. The ringed plover and grey plover, with short, thick bills, feed from the surface or in the top half-inch or so of surface mud. They hunt mainly by

119

sight, pausing motionless with head cocked before making a quick run to the prey item and grabbing it with a darting peck. They eat many small worms, *Corophium* shrimps, *Hydrobia* snails and small mud prawns and crabs. Knot and dunlin, with medium-length bills, probe in the soft mud, often immediately behind the receding tideline, pushing their bills in to full length and searching for prey by touch. The familiar redshank hunts by sight, pecking at signs of movement in the mud or probing beneath; it feeds on many crustaceans (especially *Corophium*), polychaete worms, bivalve molluscs and, once again, the ubiquitous *Hydrobia* snail.

BILLS FOR FEEDING

The long-billed waders, being larger birds, are able to exploit bigger prey items. In particular, they can probe deep down in the mud to reach the lugworms and ragworms that are unavailable to shorter-billed waders. Black-tailed godwit and bar-tailed godwit are well able to reach down in the mud to a depth of 4–5 inches, and the curlew, with the longest bill of all our shore birds, can reach another two inches or so beyond this.

The river estuaries of Britain are not only important for the hosts of wintering birds but also for other wading species, the long-distance migrants which use these rich feeding grounds as refuelling stops. Sanderling, curlew sandpiper, turnstone, ringed plover and passage dunlin, amongst others, make the long journey from the coasts of Africa to the high Arctic each spring. They cannot of course cover the journey in one flight and therefore need to rely on regular staging posts en route. Without the sanctuary and food supplies of these west European estuaries their journeys would be impossible and they could not survive. It is already believed that the numbers of many of these wader species are controlled not by the availability of suitable breeding sites but by the reliability and extent of winter feeding areas and refuelling sites.

THE OYSTERCATCHER, A SHELLFISH SPECIALIST

The oystercatcher is the most distinctive and familiar of all the waders which occur in British estuaries. Certainly there is no estuary of any substantial size which does not have oystercatchers on it at one time of year or another. These unmistakable pied birds with orange-red legs and bills are specialist feeders, requiring cockles and mussels; they congregate in very large flocks in winter on estuaries where these bivalve molluscs are numerous. Cockles are located in the wet sand by probing under the surface with the long bill. The oystercatcher then has two techniques for the difficult operation of opening the shell to get at the flesh inside. On dry sand the bird will hammer at the shell with short, powerful blows and then insert its bill to snip the adductor muscles with which the cockle keeps the two halves of its shell tightly closed. On wet sand there is a greater tendency for the birds to open the shells by stabbing the bill repeatedly in the small gap in the shell where the siphons protrude when the cockle is feeding. Once the oystercatcher has

Green sandpipers may turn up by almost any inland waterside in July and August.

inserted its bill the adductor muscles are again severed and the flesh is carefully chiselled out of one side of the valve and then the other. Mussels similarly are either stabbed or hammered depending on size, whether the substrate is hard or soft, and the preferred technique of individual birds. (Individual birds tend to specialize in one technique or the other.) Cockles and mussels are the favoured foods of oystercatchers but they eat a wide range of other shellfish at times and also crabs. Of all Britain's shore waders this is the one specialist which has learnt how to exploit the potential food resource of full-grown shellfish; only the oystercatcher with its slender but reinforced bill can produce the force required to open the hard, resilient shells. At one time, doubtless, they also fed on oysters, before their numbers declined, and this earned them their name, now something of a misnomer in Europe: across the Atlantic, however, the very similar American oystercatcher regularly feeds on oysters.

Oystercatchers are birds of the estuary tide line, specialists in shellfish exploitation.

INDUSTRIALIZED ESTUARIES

Unfortunately, estuaries are not only attractive to wildlife. They are also utilized extensively for industrial development, agricultural reclamation and other developments. Large parts of some estuaries have already been changed beyond recall, for example, those of the Thames and the Tees, but even bigger plans are threatened for the future. The possibility of further industrial (or airport) development hangs over various sites and plans for massive construction such as a barrage across the Severn estuary would change the regime of tides and mud so drastically that their effect on the huge bird flocks is impossible to predict.

It is not only the waders which feed on the vast food resources of the estuary's mud. The shelduck occurs right round the seaboard of western Europe, from Norway and the Baltic to the south coast of France. It is *par excellence* a coastal bird, dependent on the fertile, muddy waters of estuaries

Shelduck are the most typical estuary wildfowl.

THE SHELDUCK'S DIET

and low coasts for its food and its breeding sites. Together with the eider it is the only wildfowl with a strictly coastal distribution.

Food for shelduck includes a variety of small molluscs (cockles, tellins, mussels and others) and tiny crustaceans such as shrimps, prawns and sand-hoppers, but by far the most important item is the tiny snail *Hydrobia ulvae*. These small spire-shells, no bigger than grains of wheat, occur in vast numbers in the richly fertile grey mud of the estuary and form the bulk of shelduck food. Depending on where the tide is the birds feed either by scything their bills through the shallow water and liquid mud, or by head-dipping or up-ending in water up to 18 inches deep. The number of hydrobia required by the birds is prodigious and up to 3,000 individuals have been found in the stomach of one bird.

In many ways shelduck are strange members of the great wildfowl family, sharing some of the characteristics of both geese and ducks, and being placed intermediately in the classification. They have a well defined social structure with several unusual features. The open mud of the estuary is the focus of their lives; no other wildfowl depends so wholly on the animal food which develops in the fertile mud which the river supplies to the estuary.

By late February each year the shelduck pairs are re-forming within the winter flocks, renewing bonds from the previous year or initiating partnerships for the first time. It is a long while yet until egg-laying, but once paired the ducks will undertake the taxing task of establishing their own exclusive feeding areas on the muddy shore. This is a crucial time for them, when experience tells and inexperience pays heavily, for there is often insufficient space for all the would-be breeders and only those that can claim a territory, establish it and hang on to it successfully will be able to undertake nesting in late April or May. Those without a territory have nowhere to feed young and therefore can make no attempt to reproduce that year. In the shelduck's world age, aggression and experience score above youth and vitality. And so it is that the sheldrake – unlike other ducks, but in keeping with its goose relatives – has a crucial part to play throughout the whole of the breeding cycle. It is not the nest-site which is defended territory – often several pairs will nest very close together if good sites exist – but the feeding ground. Whilst the duck incubates the eggs in a rabbit burrow or a similar underground hole, the drake stoutly upholds its ownership of the feeding ground; twice a day the duck leaves the clutch to join the drake on the mud for feeding. Each time, in gentlemanly manner, the drake sees its partner home and then returns to its guard duties on the open mud.

FEEDING GROUNDS
AND FAMILY
QUARRELS

When the ducklings hatch both parents accompany them to the reserved feeding area. The female leads and the male brings up the rear as the brood is shepherded to the shore; sometimes this may mean a journey of half a mile or a mile from the nest-site – a journey fraught with dangers until the tiny ducklings are safely on the open shore.

Shelduck are quarrelsome and aggressive birds and there are frequent skirmishes between family groups. The female initiates many of these encounters and boundary disputes, lowering her head and neck horizontally to point at a supposed intruder, thereby galvanizing the drake into action. The drake signals its intent with jerky bowing movements of the head and then launches itself into headlong pursuit. During these continual scuffles and skirmishes different broods of ducklings frequently become wholly confused as each one rushes to the sanctuary of the nearest adult it can find. Thus some pairs may be seen with 15–20 young whilst others have only one or two.

MOULTING ACROSS
THE NORTH SEA

This confusion is of little account or consequence because by now the adult birds are beginning to moult their body feathers and in early July another phenomenon of the shelduck's world takes place. The adult birds gather into loose flocks, leaving all the half-grown ducklings in the charge of one or two 'nurse' adults and then, in one non-stop flight, they cross right over the North Sea to the vast flats of the Knechtsand on the Wadenzee off the coast of West Germany. This is where virtually the entire population of shelduck from north-western Europe congregate to moult their flight feathers and where they will remain, flightless for four weeks or so, until the new feathers are fully grown. Here British birds meet with others from the Baltic, Ireland, Scandinavia, Germany and the Low Countries, to form one vast throng of 100,000 or more shelduck. Not until September does the flock start to break up and the birds make a leisurely return to their breeding areas.

There is only one other moulting area for adults in the whole of north-west Europe and that is on the shallow flats of Bridgewater Bay on the outer reaches of the Severn, where 3,000–4,000 birds, probably of Irish origin, congregate for the late-summer moult.

The shelduck nest on the marsh edge or in the immediate hinterland. Here they are safe from inundation by high 'spring' tides (a factor which limits the number of birds which use the estuaries for breeding). Added to this vulnerability to flooding is the fact that the breeding habitat is restricted to sites on the ground: for these reasons breeding birds are not numerous.

Redshank are the noisiest and most conspicuous of estuary birds in summer. They breed on the upper salt-marshes; 'watchdogs' of the estuary, they are the first to raise the alarm when intruders cross the marsh. Lesser numbers of lapwing, snipe and oystercatchers also breed on many of the estuaries, while skylarks are often abundant and on the highest areas of marsh pairs of yellow wagtails and reed buntings may be found.

On some of the bigger estuaries colonies of black-headed gulls and terns still occur, albeit in decreasing numbers. A few decades ago on finger-blowing days in winter the vast marshes of the Solway wedged between the rivers Esk and Eden echoed to the massed cries of wild geese, the sky full of skeins that plied between the marshes and the Scottish coast, and thronged with wheeling, twisting flocks of bar-tailed godwits, moving in unimagined high-speed synchrony, and pulsing flocks of curlew, dunlin and knot on the marsh's far reaches. In summer the cattle-full marshes were an idyll of space, warmth, sunshine, colour and birds. Birds, it seemed, nested everywhere. Amongst the sheets of sea pink oystercatchers and lapwing nested. The incessant alarm calls of redshank accompanied every moment one spent on the marsh. Dunlin nests could be found, too, more difficult to find even than skylarks', in unexpected tufts of grass. Loose colonies of gulls spread over parts of the marsh – a nest at the base of every one of the tall posts dotted over it – remnants of those erected to protect the British from German glider landings. Far out on the marsh terns nested, both Arctic and common; theirs were the most exciting of all nests to find: one after another in little hollows in the sea of thrift, scurvy grass and purslane. The agitated birds filled the air as one passed – a buoyant, piercing, snow-white blizzard.

On a small estuary in the west the tide is on the turn and the boats at anchor in the distance swing on their moorings to face the open sea and the incoming waters. It is late afternoon at the end of winter. A dense, noisy flock of starlings feeding busily on the upper saltings leaps suddenly to life and rises high above the marsh in a tight pack. Nearby lapwing and a spring of teal also scatter as the sickle shape of the hunting peregrine passes over the marsh; they are lucky, for it has none of them in its sights this time. It curves across the saltings to land on the whitened hulk of an old tree swept down by the river in flood and now stranded on the marsh. This estuary has been the winter home for the peregrine and will continue to be so for a week or two longer before it returns to the hills above to breed.

BREEDING BIRDS
ON THE SUMMER
MARSHES

Sea-swallows – common terns – are buoyant and agile on the wing.

**BIRD PREDATORS
ON THE MARSH
FLOCKS**

The estuary marshes are rich hunting grounds for birds of prey. Although this estuary is small another peregrine also appears here regularly as do two or three different merlins and a hen harrier. The merlins – and sparrowhawks from the adjacent farmland – maraud the flocks of finches, starlings and thrushes on the drier parts of the marsh while the peregrine terrify the flocks of ducks and waders farther out. The deft and graceful hen harrier feeds mainly on voles and other small mammals in the rough grasses in the upper parts of the marsh but is never averse to seizing small birds if they can be taken by surprise. Short-eared owls also occur occasionally and on many estuaries are regular winter visitors; they too feed principally on small mammals.

Once the danger of the passing peregrine has gone the starlings, lapwings and teal settle again and start to feed. The estuary and its marshes are quiet and still again in the brilliant evening light with the sun low over the sea. This is a relatively small estuary, three miles or so in length and with high hills sweeping down to its margins on the north and south, and although it possesses an atmosphere of expectation and excitement, commonly produced by bigger estuaries, it also has an intimacy of its own. The quarter mile of saltings stretching to the river channel look flat and empty, save that they are dotted with time-worn posts, the inevitable, randomly-placed ornaments of all such marshes. They throw long shadows on the grass. The sward of the marsh has a frosted appearance in parts where last year's dead fronds are still showing through the new growth of grass. Clumps of rushes, too, and tussocks of grasses stand out pale in the evening light. In the middle distance the lower saltings have a gingery hue enhanced by the low sunlight. These are the beds of spartina, an invasive plant which colonizes the open mud, building up the silt around it and rapidly reducing the areas of open ground. The marsh appears bowling-green flat from a distance but in reality it is broken up by

Wildfowl waders and birds of prey are the predominant groups on the estuary.

narrow, twisting, muddy creeks, shallow pans of water and low hollows which mark the lines of former creeks. It seems there are few birds on the marsh, but this too is deceptive. Wigeon call from the fold where they are feeding; similarly, a curlew appears, followed by another, walking on to higher ground. A redshank rises from a creek and flies to the river bank; it passes over a group of curlew resting motionless and unnoticed. The longer one looks at the marsh the more it reveals: mallard (in pairs now and shortly to start nesting), shelduck similarly paired, a group of meadow pipits, and a party of teal which rise from one hidden pool of water and drop on to another.

This marsh is in fact full of birds, as are the marshes within all our estuaries. These, the most productive sections of any rivers, provide the boundless source of food for the throngs of birds at the river's mouth. The river's course is run now, its energy spent and its priceless cargo of fertility delivered and spread in the estuary to maintain it as one of the richest environments on earth.

THE HERON, RIVER BIRD FROM SOURCE TO SEA

Under the slender span of the Severn bridge the Wye and the Severn join once more at the end of their separate courses from Plynlimon to the sea; they meet here in what is, suitably, the largest of British estuaries, the Bristol Channel. Below the bridge the waters are brown and dangerous in the swirling channels between the sandbanks. In the half light of a grey evening the black silhouette of a heron beats its way slowly and purposefully across the estuary. On bowed wings with head drawn in and legs extended it labours against the wind, wing tips just above the rippling water. With a final glide it rises on to the rocks beside the river edge. It folds its wings, shakes itself and stands hunched but comfortable and well fed: the heron and the river in inseparable harmony. The heron was there at the birth of the river on the desolate bogs and moors of Plynlimon; it fished in the upland stream, bred beside the fertile lowland river and was not intimidated by the urban stretches. Now, at the end of the river's course, the heron is present at its departure to the sea, symbolizing more than any other bird the union between the river and its wildlife.

INDEX

SELECT BIBLIOGRAPHY

Boag, D., *The Kingfisher*, Blandford Press, 1982
Cramp, S., *et al, Birds of the Western Palearctic*, vols. I–III, Oxford University Press, 1977–83
Davies, N. B., 'Territorial Behaviour of Pied Wagtails in Winter', *British Birds*, 75: 261–267, 1982
London Bird Reports, 1981 and 1982
Macan, T. T. and Worthington, E. B., *Life in Lakes and Rivers*, New Naturalist series, Collins, 1951
Mead, C. J., 'Colony fidelity in Sand Martins', *Bird Study*, 26: 99–106, 1979

Montier, D. (editor), *Atlas of Breeding Birds of the London Area*, Batsford, 1977
N.C.C., *Lead Poisoning in Swans*, 1981
Prater, A. J., *Estuary Birds of Britain and Ireland*, T. & A. D. Poyser, 1981
Sharrock, J. T. R., *Atlas of Breeding Birds in Britain and Ireland*, BTO/IWC, 1976